The Poetry of Charles Olson

Also by Thomas F. Merrill:

William Perkins: 1558–1602 (ed.)
Allen Ginsberg
Christian Criticism: A Study of Literary God-talk

The Poetry of Charles Olson

A PRIMER

Thomas F. Merrill

NEWARK: UNIVERSITY OF DELAWARE PRESS
LONDON AND TORONTO:
ASSOCIATED UNIVERSITY PRESSES

Associated University Presses, Inc.
4 Cornwall Drive
East Brunswick, N.J. 08816

Associated University Presses Ltd
27 Chancery Lane
London WC2A 1NS, England

Associated University Presses
Toronto M5E 1A7, Canada

Library of Congress Cataloging in Publication Data

Merrill, Thomas F.
  The poetry of Charles Olson.

  Bibliography: p.
  Includes index.
  1. Olson, Charles, 1910–1970—Criticism and
interpretation.   I. Title.
PS3529.L655Z77   1982   811'.54   81-50341
ISBN 0-87413-196-0   AACR2

Printed in the United States of America

Contents

To another Charles
who also seeks "that which is most familiar"

Preface

The reputation of Charles Olson has finally matured from an aberrant curiosity to an academic fact of life. He has an archive, a curator, a scholarly journal, and now a growing number of books devoted to his life and works. His enthusiasts have effectively established him as an influential and apparently enduring presence in postmodernist poetic theory. The thrust of his cultural position has been outlined by Sherman Paul's *Olson's Push* and the legitimacy of his aesthetic theory and technique handsomely explored by Robert von Hallberg in *The Scholar's Art*. George Butterick's *A Guide to the Maximus Poems* now reduces the forbidding allusiveness of that equivalent of the epic to at least a negotiable challenge for the bemused reader. Charles Olson's academic shrine has an impressive foundation.

The poetry itself may be another matter. What strikes readers as palatably plausible in the brash, curmudgeonly prose of "Projective Verse" (Olson's "white paper" on poetics) may in the raw actuality of the naked poem, divested of theoretical cover, prove less digestible. Some exegetical seasoning may be called for, which this book presumes to provide. It is, in other words, a labor of hermeneutical midwifery that, alas, is guilty of a measure of obstetrical violence in its zeal to deliver Olson's obscurities to light—violence, because its only alternative to silence is to traffic in traditional methods of explication that violate the very principles of "projective" art. It must try to explain, for example, when it ought simply to experience; it reflects on the reader's response when response alone is all that is called for; it worries about "difficulties" in the poems when Olson insists they should be left to lie. In short, it is an apologetics, an effort to present Olson's poetry to readers as yet uncommitted to its presuppositions. As such, it achieves only the crudest counterfeitings of the "CELEBRATION OF THE ACTUAL" that Olson defines as his "ART." And yet, such counterfeitings (call them benevolent frauds) may be justified, given the interpretive challenge the poems pose, if only to lure the curious reader to tryst where, prepared for the encounter, he can arrange affairs on his own.

The procedure of the book is simple. Chapter 1 tries to engineer an evocation of Olson as literary "phenomenon," academic maverick, avant-garde theorist-poet, scholarly "industry" and vulnerable human being in ascent and decline. Using Black Mountain College as a point of reference, it attempts to "place" Olson within the literary and scholarly spectrum of the fifties and sixties. Since Olson's philosophical commitments dictate his use of language, chapter 2 discusses how the apparent "illiteracy" (Olson's word) of projective writing is actually the deliberate consequence of a structural accommodation of language to an underlying ontology. It seeks to convey a *comprehensive* sense of the implications built into the term *projective verse* and the slogan *FORM IS NEVER MORE THAN AN EXTENSION OF CONTENT.*

The remaining chapters examine the individual poems themselves. Chapter 3 takes the early "The Kingfishers" and regards it as a model projective enterprise—pure Olson in concentrate. It tries to relate as exhaustively as possible the theory discussed in chapter 2 to its practical outcome in the poem. Chapter 4 undertakes a close reading of the poems in Olson's earliest major collection, *The Distances*, attempting to demonstrate how they support Olson's Herodotean conviction that "we have been estranged from that with which we are most familiar." That discussion is continued in chapter 5 with the poems in *Archaeologist of Morning*, a collection of all the poems Olson authorized for publication exclusive of the *Maximus* sequence.

Finally, the *Maximus* poems are discussed in chapters 6 and 7 as a major attempt to delineate the formal nature of the American long poem, the New World equivalent to the epic. Here the focus is less on the individual poems of the sequence (although as many as feasible are exposed to explication), but instead on the development of Olson's sense of the mythological mode of epic expression.

I wish to acknowledge my gratitude to George Butterick, curator of the Charles Olson Archives at the University of Connecticut, for his unfailing hospitality and helpful suggestions, as well as the Estate of Charles Olson for permission to quote from *The Distances, Maximus IV, V, VI, The Maximus Poems: Volume Three*, and unpublished material from the Archives at the University of Connecticut Library. I thank Corinth Books for permission to quote from *The Maximus Poems*, Viking Penguin for permission to include excerpts from *Archaeologist of Morning*, and the Board of Regents of the University of Wisconsin for permission to reprint the material in chapter 3 that originally appeared in *Contemporary Literature* (17 [1976]: 506–28). My gratitude also extends to the University of Delaware Research Fund for its financial support of the project, and to Mrs. Rita Beasley for her painstaking skill and patience in typing and proofreading the manuscript.

Key to Frequently Cited Matrials

AM   *Archaeologist of Morning* (London: Cape Goliard Press/Grossman Publishers, 1970).

AP   *Additional Prose*, ed. George Butterick (Bolinas: Four Seasons Foundation, 1974).

CtU   Charles Olson Archives, University of Connecticut.

HU   *Human Universe and Other Essays*, ed. Donald Allen (New York: Grove Press, 1967).

LO   *Letters for Origin: 1950–1955*, ed. Albert Glover (London: Cape Goliard Press/Grossman Publishers, 1969).

M   *The Maximus Poems* (New York: Jargon/Corinth Press, 1960).

M2   *Maximus Poems IV, V, VI* (London: Cape Goliard Press/Grossman Publishers, 1968).

M3   *The Maximus Poems: Volume Three*, ed. Charles Boer and George Butterick (New York: Grossman Publishers, 1975).

ML   *Mayan Letters*, ed. Robert Creeley (London: Jonathan Cape, 1968).

PT   *Poetry and Truth: The Beloit Lectures and Poems*, ed. George Butterick (San Francisco: Four Seasons Foundation, 1971).

SVH   *The Special View of History*, ed. Ann Charters (Berkeley, Calif.: Oyez, 1970).

1

Charles Olson: The Ultimate Adam

"This is civilization, the whole state
of things," he said pointing to his guts.
—Robert Duncan

Black Mountain College lived for twenty-three years in the
mountains of North Carolina as a small, desperately poor,
unaccredited institution totally committed to teaching and
the arts. Regularly breathing in and out such luminaries as
Josef and Anni Albers, Merce Cunningham, John Cage,
Buckminster Fuller, Robert Duncan, Robert Creeley,
Franz Kline, and Willem de Kooning, to name but a few, it
was, as Martin Duberman puts it, "unified by little more
than a disdain for life as usually lived and some unsettling
notions—sometimes confused and self-glamorizing,
sometimes startlingly courageous—as to how it might be
made better."[1] It was an undisciplined, self-consciously
intellectual, and committed community that was more
than occasionally brushed by genius. It stands as an emblem for its last rector and its last owner,[2] Charles Olson,
whose teaching, writing, and literary reputation bear witness to the irony of how much, in a larger sense, Black
Mountain truly "owned" him.

Black Mountain and Charles Olson project one another.
Not "Black Mountain" as that loose constellation of poets
(Creeley, Blackburn, Levertov, Duncan, etc.) who found
its father figure in Olson, nor "Black Mountain" as the
short-lived *Review* that blossomed in the soil of his projectivist dogmas, nor even the College itself over whose demise he presided in its last tense years. No, the words *Black
Mountain* project Olson because they imprint on all they
touch the hallmark of an attitude, a perspective, a "stance"
("I teach posture," Olson once declared[3]) that literary
"school," magazine, College, and man all share. That

"stance" dictates almost every paragraph of the *Black Mountain College Catalogue*:

> ...ideas are only such as they exist in things and in actions.... it is not things in themselves but *what happens between things* where the life of them is to be sought. Our central and consistent effort is to teach method, not content; to emphasize process.... The law of the teacher at Black Mountain is to function as a working "artist" ... to be no passive recipient or hander-out of mere information.
>
> There is a technic to be learned, a grammar of the art of living and working in the world. Logic, as severe as can be, must be learned; if for no other reason, to know its limitations.... There are subtle means of communication that have been lost by mankind, as our nerve ends have been cauterized by schooling. To learn to move, at least without fear, to fear, see, touch, also without fear ... to be aware of everything around us ... this is to start to penetrate the past and to *feel* as well as mentally see our way into the future.[4]

Only a few of these words are Olson's. Most were written by Black Mountain's founder, John A. Rice, but they could easily be smuggled into "Projective Verse," "The Human Universe," or any other random specimen of Olson's prose without causing the slightest ripple. There is the repudiation of ideas in favor of actions and things, which establishes Olson's link to the Pound-Williams tradition. There are the numerous reverberations of Alfred North Whitehead's philosophy of organism, particularly in the emphasis upon process over substance, "between-ness" over inert matter, and "feeling"[5] over logic. That logic must be learned "to know its limitations" reflects Olson's faith in Keats's "negative capability": "when a man is capable of being in uncertainties, Mysteries and doubts, without any irritable reaching after fact and reason."[6] There is the overt bias that traditional "schooling" (with its Aristotelian presuppositions) indeed has "cauterized" not only our metaphysical assumptions but the very conduct of our language as well. In short, the aims of Black Mountain and the aims of Charles Olson are indistinguishable. Duberman feels that "Charles Olson was unquestionably the heartbeat of Black Mountain during its last five years,"[7] but he might well have added that, in its own unique way, Black Mountain was the heartbeat of Olson until the end of his life.

We hear of him as an eccentric postmodernist poet, a murky theoretical standard-bearer for the Pound-Williams wing of American poetry, a fatherly magnet for après-Beat sensitivities, the Maximus behind the legendary *Maximus Poems*. But what was he really like? As with some cheeses, the firsthand accounts of the man tend to ripen far too quickly into legend to be very reliable so that the imposing shadow of "Maximus" too often blurs our perception of Charles. One place to begin might be Fielding Dawson's first impression that he wrote down in a letter to his sister as an eighteen-year-old newcomer to Black Mountain:

He is . . . gosh, words fail me . . . about ten steps higher than stupendous. He is about six feet eight or nine and has shoulders like an ox. He must weigh about two hundred and sixty or seventy. He eats, well, let me tell you about last night's meal. . . .

On the table was a plate that has about five hot dogs on it. Another plate had about ten buns, another had heaping piles of tomatoes and lettuce, and then there was another that was stacked high with potatoe [*sic*] chips and oh so many more food.

When I left, everything was gone except a few pieces of casual leftover lettuce bits. He thrust his face within about six inches of the girl who he was talking to . . . picks up a hot dog, breaks it in half, smears one end in a mess of mustard on his plate, takes a bun rips it in two and then into quarters and then into very small bits. He takes a gargantuan bite of the hot dog, crams a bit of bun in, reaches across the table, grabs a slice of nice red tomatoe [*sic*], bites down on it and his paw returns with little pale red drippings of what once was a tomatoe. Then he scrapes up a few fingers full of potatoe chips

and he squeezes these in his mouth. Then another bite
of the hot dog, etc . . . All this time telling about Howard
Fast, [Saroyan], Ezra Pound, T S. Eliot, Thomas
Wolfe . . . etc . . . and smoking a cigarette and drinking a
glass of milk![8]

Even taking adolescent impressionability into account,
Dawson's portrait-in-process is a vivid index to the whole
of Olson. He was a furious ingester of not only food but
reading material as well. Barriers between mental and
physical experience, just as between Eliot and hot dogs,
simply did not exist. Olson's "paws" appropriated anything
and everything in the flux about him that he designated as
useful, and he did it at typewriter, as at table, with a kind
of messy, direct grab. This visceral and cerebral foraging
continued to his very end in 1970. Recalling Olson (as his
houseguest) in the sad, final year of his life, Charles Boer
reports,

> I remember well that first night, after you had finally
> gone to bed . . . hearing you in the next room furiously
> turning the pages of books, munching vigorously on the
> lettuce and the other food. Every few hours that night I
> was suddenly awakened by a new burst of frantic
> munching and page-turning. It went on all night.[9]

Body and soul at table together. That is Olson and that is
Black Mountain, too. No "partitioning" of reality for
either. No false walls between things, no artificial doors.
Pages, lettuce, Eliot, hot dogs, Jung, and baseball—the ultimate interdisciplinary existence.

But a man who deliberately violates boundaries, who
methodically blurs "literary" issues by testing them against
the axioms of quantum physics, topology, and even archeology, who pays qualified homage to Pound and Williams but prefers the nourishment of Whitehead, Jung,
Sauer, Frobenius, and Riemann, who, on top of it all, is as
boorishly dogmatic as any against whom he raves, such a
man can hardly expect the kind of wide acclaim that one
senses he coveted throughout his career. He attracted in-

stead a kind of cult following that drew as easily from academia as it did from bohemia. With his scholarly credentials and enormous range of reading, Olson lent intellectual respectability to otherwise suspect postmodernist trends. With disdain for classical logic and "Euclidean" rigidities, he energetically tried to break down disciplinary walls, particularly walls that traditionally have separated science and literature. He moved as freely and confidently in physics as he did poetry, with Einstein as with Shakespeare, with politicians as well as with Beatniks. Like the poetic form he evangelized in "Projective Verse," Olson himself was open to the whole front of experience from which he drew his considerable, though not always understood, strengths.

Some random assessments suggest the broad range of reaction Olson's work and person provoke. John Cage, himself a controversial former colleague at Black Mountain, predictably found Olson "just as sweet and lovely as a little dog,"[10] but a more conservatively oriented student saw him as

> basically a charlatan. In thought and teaching he is a faddish member of the New York and Washington *avant garde*. I neither liked nor respected him.[11]

Olson's own former teacher and friend, Edward Dahlberg, dubbed him

> the stuffed Cyclops of Gloucester... a refrigerated verser... a knave. He had noble brows. But his stature was his shame.... He had an ungovernable impulse to destroy himself.... I shall always love Charles Olson and condemn him.[12]

His poetics evoked similarly disparate reactions. Some felt his theories (largely as they were expressed in "Projective Verse")

> encouraged the renewal of formal experimentation discouraged during the years of the conservative counter-

revolution; it was Olson speaking out at a crucial time who provided a catalyst for the work of the rising generation of poets.[13]

but others seem convinced that the essay offered "nothing more than a number of exhortations to write good verse with few rules or characteristics emerging" and that the notion of "open verse" accomplished only a "creative irresponsibility with the semblance of a rationale which may be defended in heated and cloudy terms by its supposed practitioners."[14]

Even those who found "Projective Verse" a fresh and exciting theoretical manifesto had trouble with Olson's verse. It is decidedly an acquired taste. Robert Duncan, who eventually was to say, "He was a poet, a poet like I had not seen in all my life. . . . Olson was to become *my* poet,"[15] recalls his first encounter with Olson's verse, a response he undoubtedly shares with many other readers:

> So he sends me *Y & X*. I don't know if you know what *Y & X* was, but it was like his first thing in poetry; . . . and I said "What's this?" and I tried to read this *Y & X* and I said "Oh, for Christ's sake, I can't make anything out of this," and I threw it in the wastepaper basket, where a book today worth twenty million dollars is floating away down the river to somewhere.[16]

Olson draws strong responses from friend and foe, which is a good indication that he works close to the nerve of the body poetic. One characterization of Olson's literary impact, from the *Times Literary Supplement*, stresses his rebellious mien and then goes on to make this pertinent generalization:

> . . . it is the rebels whose work evinces an almost overwhelming preoccupation with style, with diction, with admissible or inadmissible ways of composing poetry and in nearly every case, a rigid dogmatism about what may or may not be allowed. The poetry of revolt is in fact the poetry of a new formalism.[17]

Olson *is* a rebel, he *is* preoccupied with style, and *is* rigidly dogmatic about what may or may not be allowed in verse. The unremitting pressure of his formalist dogma can be detected in every bullish, arrogant, often maudlin guise in his remarkably revealing correspondence to the patiently beleaguered, fledgling editor of *Origin*, Cid Corman. In these letters Olson does not limit his formalist preoccupations to his own contributions to the magazine but literally browbeats, even blackmails, Corman into conceiving *Origin* as an extension of his own arbitrary "projective" views. He demands, for example, that the first issue devote forty (later fifty) pages to the correspondence and "finished work" of one Charles Olson, justifying that demand on the following principles:

> 1—it has nothing to do, actually, with Olson: it has to do with a process of *fronting* to the *whole* front of reality *as it now presents itself*
> 2—it rests (such 40 pages, *with* correspondence) on a premise that no such confrontation can be done by
>> (a) the old deductive premise of form—and that goes for *poems* as well as *essays* as well as *stories* (mark you)
>> (b) that art & culture are somehow separated from the other planes of energy on which a people express themselves (economics, politics, films, television, or whatever "entertainment")
>> (c) that life (what is "human") is an absolute instead of—what I think I am not at all alone in taking it—that is, specifically, "Life," that dirty capital (doric, corinthian OR iambic)—IS RELATIVE to conditions of REALITY (as distinguished from, as *ahead* of life "human life," at any given time::: life, in this sense, is a stop to consolidate gains already being pushed beyond by the reality instant to you or to any man who is pushing (*LO*, 5)

When Corman demurs, Olson doggedly holds fast:

> my dear duckweed:
>   each sentence you write breaks my

heart. it is as simple as that. so let's be practical: (1) can you, will you, by some means (even a notary, maybe!) give me absolute assurance you will (despite all weathers, fair or foul) give me the 40 pages of issue #1 you have told you plan to give me? ... (You will see how, it is, almost, like a book, such a block, and yet, the beauty of it, is, it is not a book, it is a magazine, and does, therefore, allow, precisely, the sort of composing by discontinuity, non-deduction, field, fragment, grit & vulgarity, that, at root, can make a magazine, today, fresh. (*LO*, 12)

Behind the bluster lies a literary integrity that Olson never consciously violated. In magazine or in poem the whole front of reality must be met, and fresh, without stale deduction. But where does such uncompromising self-assurance come from? What is the source of Olson's patent willful obstinacy? Paradoxically, it comes from obedience. Olson was an obedient man and an obedient writer. "The mark of life," he was fond of saying, "is that what we obey is who and what we are,"[18] and this premise dictated his writing no less than his living. His passivity to forces external to his consciousness is reflected in such remarks as "I don't know what I'm up to. And I must stay in that state in order to accomplish what I have to do."[19]

Olson's obedience is as mysterious and potent as faith. During his life he tended to express it in terms of his particular interests at the moment. Describing how he came to write his study of *Moby-Dick, Call Me Ishmael*, for example, Olson said,

It started, for me, from a sensing of something I found myself obeying for sometime before.... It got itself put down as *space*, a factor of experience I took as of such depth, width, and intensity that, unwittingly, I insisted upon it as fact.[20]

Later, in an essay called "The Gate and the Center" (*HU*, 17–23), obedience took the form of a cultural imperative called the "will to cohere." In "Projective Verse" he advised poets to make the line obedient to "breath" (*HU*, 54), and

in "The Kingfishers" (*D*, 5–11) he enlisted Norbert
Wiener's "feedback" principle to illustrate the mechanics
of man's properly obedient stance toward reality. Ultimately he was to find in Whitehead's concept of "creative
advance" the metaphysical sanction for how, as a writer,
you can "leap upon yourself before you know who you
are."[21]

Amid these progressive articulations of obedience—
"space," the "will to cohere," "breath," "feedback," and
"creative advance"—there is one abiding constant: Olson's
blind faith in the urgings of what he once called the "life in
us."[22] This is not necessarily *our own life* in us, but an authority that is reliably "other" and accessible simply by our
acknowledgment that we are "held in the hands of nature"
(*HU*, 11), that is, obedient—unwilling to impose our assertive will upon her. In exchange for our faith in this "life in
us" we are promised the "secrets objects share," "dimensions larger than the man," and "projective size" (*HU*, 60).

The obedient stance, then, is a repudiation of ego-
consciousness, but it is not, as Robert Bly charges, simply a
case of Olson's "restating Eliot's belief in the desirability of
'extinguishing the personality.'"[23] Olson indeed wants to
"wash the ego out in its own 'bath'(os)" (*AP*, 17), but in his
lexicon "ego" and "personality" are quite different things.
Ego is precisely why "Eliot is *not* projective" (*HU*, 61). For
Eliot, the ego is "the mind alone, and a scholastic mind at
that" (*HU*, 61). It is Eliot's conscious mind as interfering
ego that makes it impose its organizing will on reality
rather than remaining obedient to it. The "personality,"
on the other hand, is inextinguishable in Olson and his
work, and what is so different about Olson's attitude toward it is that he locates it not, as Eliot does, in the mind,
or even in the soul, but in the physical body where its
proprioceptive energies pick up "knowledge" of a different nature than that picked up by the conscious ego
through the five senses. This is why Olson insists in "The
Human Universe" and elsewhere that what we receive
from within is as epistemologically significant as what we
take in from without (*HU*, 9–10). The bodily sense of

things—proprioception—is, in other words, the seat of a
personality that possesses a distinct "otherness" in respect
to the conscious ego—a "personality" that can command
obedience. Olson once put it this way: " . . . what you find
yrself doing, is establishing yr own self as the rail."[24]

A man's obligation, particularly if he is a writer, is to
keep his rail free and clear of debris, that is, to prevent the
"lyrical interference of the individual as ego" (*HU*, 59)
from rendering him "estranged from that with which he is
most familiar" (*SVH*, 14). This means that such construc-
tions of the ego as metaphysical systems, logic, classification, abstractions, ideal forms, symbols, similes, allegory,
comparison—all that is *referential* to reality rather than *of*
it—must be purged. The anthropological first principle of
the ego—that man is "Lord of Creation"—must be dismissed in favor of the dogma of "physicality"[25]—that man
is a bodily fellow-traveler, a concomitant entity, among the
other entities that make up that process which is reality.

Olson's otherwise eccentric life begins to take on a
coherence when it is appraised in terms of his obedience to
his "own self as the rail." A passage from his poem
"Maximus, to Himself" serves as a rough blueprint for a
biography:

> I have had to learn the simplest things
> last. Which made for difficulties.
> Even at sea I was slow, to get the hand out, or to cross
> a wet deck.
>   The sea was not, finally, my trade.
> But even my trade, at it, I stood estranged
> from that which was most familiar. Was delayed,
> and not content with the man's argument
> that such postponement
> is now the nature of
> obedience,
>   that we are all late
>   in a slow time,
>   that we grow up many
>   And the single
>   is not easily
>   known

It could be, though the sharpness (the *achiote*)
I note in others,
makes more sense
than my own distances. The agilities
                    they show daily
                    who do the world's
                    businesses
                    And who do nature's
                    as I have no sense
                    I have done either
I have made dialogues,
have discussed ancient texts,
have thrown what light I could, offered
what pleasures
doceat allows
                    But the known?
This, I have had to be given,
a life, love, and from one man
the world.

                                        (*M*, 52)

The difficulty of working down to the simplicities of life
was Olson's most persistent epistemological exasperation.
It crowded his life from its beginning (Worcester, Massachusetts, December 27, 1910) until his death in New
York Hospital in 1970. He saw his growth as perversely
backward, from complex to simple, from strange to familiar, from theory to the hard, thumping reality of a "wet
deck." His constant goal, the "familiar," lurked irritatingly
out of reach, particularly during those years he was, as he
put it, being "uneducated" at Wesleyan University (B.A.,
1932; M.A., 1933), Yale, and Harvard. The "delay" he
speaks of, the "postponement" of his encounter with the
"familiar," he attributes to the nature of obedience, as if
his estrangement were an obligatory apprenticeship before initiation into authentic experience. Logic, as the
College Catalogue counsels, "must be learned . . . to know
its limitations."

It was probably the wet deck of the fishing vessel *Doris
M. Hawes* that first made Olson so physically aware of his
estrangement. During the summer after his first year of

teaching at Clark University, he signed on for a swordfishing cruise into the North Atlantic. Except for summer jobs with Gorton-Pew on the wharves at Gloucester and with the Post Office, Olson's life had been largely academic and quite theoretical. His acomplishments included his master's thesis, "The Growth of Herman Melville, Prose Writer and Poetic Thinker," and the very considerable feat of unearthing Melville's private library, but his experience on board the *Doris M. Hawes* was an encounter with a very different kind of reality that made him aware of his cumbersome ineptitude in the work-a-day world of the "familiar." Olson assessed his own capabilities against the practical, familiar skills of seamen and, as the poem abundantly shows, he felt discomfort. The journal that he kept on board ship reveals an almost sentimental hero-worship of the "sharpness" these fishermen exhibited daily:

> Fishermen are, like gulls, tough ones. There's a muscularity about them, not of the biceps, but of the whole stuff of man, the gut. . . . There's a command and thus a dignity about them over this thing we introverts grapple for and miss and call life; they don't bother to name it but they've got it.[26]

The journal also poignantly records the "estrangement":

> . . . the more I read & write, the less I'm liked by these men, men who respect the hand more than the mind, so that a boy of 14 who whittles out a model of a vessel is more to be liked than a boy of 24 who listens & is sometimes seen writing in a notebook suspiciously, quietly.[27]

This awareness of two worlds—the theoretical and the "familiar"—nettled Olson to the end and rendered him a kind of perpetually displaced person. His cranky hostility to most of the academic establishment came from his opinion that they may think but they do not *do*. His intellectual Olympus, elaborately rostered in "A Bibliography of America for Ed Dorn,"[28] is notably peopled by men who, though academics, are nevertheless "doers" who are very much familiar with wide varieties of wet decks. As an academician himself at Black Mountain, Olson pushed the idea of "shops"—working, producing, teaching ate-liers—as a means to complement the classroom. Even in the classroom, however, it was Herodotus's activist histori-cal method that set the tone: *'istorin*, finding out for one-self.[29]

Finding out for oneself was a principle that generated Olson's own work, too. We see it in his remarkable coup in ferreting out the Melville library. "No one but Olson," Charles Boer reports, "who scribbles information endlessly in his own books, would think of such a project."[30] Some of the flavor of the chase remains in Olson's recollection of the enterprise:

> ... in one of the finest slickest iced countrysides I ever knew Edward Matthews & I drove to East Orange, New Jersey and came away, at the end of a Sunday after-noon, with 95 volumes of that library including the Shakespeare! (One of his granddaughters)
>
> I may already have set out to retrace the sale. In any case the spring of '34—I was then 23—I succeeded. It was John Anderson (who had, in 1891, been a booksel-ler, but the founder, afterwards, of the Anderson Gal-leries, now Parke-Bernet ...) He was the one who put me on to Oscar Wegalin, who had then—in 1891—been his delivery boy.[31]

This thirst for personal involvement in the most physically active sense, even in the most "intellectual" projects, was later to lure Olson to Mexico where, under the baking sun, he crawled and scrambled through Mayan ruins and at-tempted to live *en famille* with the residue of that ancient culture for the purpose of confirming that amalgam of Fenollosa, Jung, Brooks Adams, and Jane Harrison that he was beginning to define as his "stance towards reality." In his writing and his life things had to be real, not refer-ential to reality.

Before the Mexican expedition, however, Olson's ap-prenticeship took him to Washington. He had finished his sojourn at Clark in 1936 and had gone to Harvard as a graduate student in English and American Literature. Although he finally completed all the course work for the Ph.D., the lure of "doing" presented itself in the form of a Guggenheim fellowship for Melville studies. He left Harvard.

During this time his influential association with Edward Dahlberg flourished. Dahlberg describes their relationship with all the drama of a Greek tragedy:

> Around 1938, when I was living in East Gloucester, an obscure youth came to my door and introduced himself as Charles Olson. He was the son of a Swedish mailcarrier and an Irish Catholic mother.... Soon I gave him complete devotion, immolating my own interests to his advantage. I published his essay, "Lear and Moby Dick," in *Twice a Year*, opposing a lioness with barking dogs for a belly to do it. Olson had two staunch friends who helped him: I and Charles Olson.... Olson's fervor for me ebbed, and I saw his scab of pride, the fleas of envy biting his entrails, and the putrid smoke of his jealousy..... Then one day he came to me, his head pained, the broad surfaces of his face gnarled and warped, and disclosed that he feared my influence was impeding him.... Charles Olson abolished the memory of himself and me, hurling the latter, his monitor, into the gullet of Cocytus.[32]

Obviously both Olson and Dahlberg took themselves very seriously. Although Dahlberg may have considered himself Olson's "monitor," it is evident in hindsight that Olson's obedience was committed elsewhere. Olson was under considerable stress. He had become very tense and exhausted over repeated attempts to revise his "Lear and Moby Dick" manuscript for *Twice-a-Year* and, according to Boer, "his nerves give way altogether and he enters a hospital in Boston for a rest. He leaves Harvard for good.... The life of an academician is not for Olson."[33]

This is certainly not a conventional academician. The Guggenheim bore fruit as a manuscript of over 400 pages that Dahlberg convinced him not to publish because the style was "too Hebraic, Biblical Old Testament."[34] Ironically, five years later a completely rewritten version of it, *Call Me Ishmael*, would be rejected by T. S. Eliot on the grounds that it was "too little, and too American a book."[35]

In the meantime, Olson took a job as publicity director for the ACLU in New York and married Constance Mathilde Wilcock. The young couple moved to Washington in 1942 so that Charles could begin a two-year association with the Office of War Information. Ultimately he rose to the position of associate chief, Foreign Language Division, before moving on to the Directorship of the Foreign Nationalities Division of the Democratic National Committee. Says Boer: "He is becoming 'established,' President Roosevelt likes him."[36]

But Roosevelt died and Olson's political enthusiasm died with him. The "rail" on which his obedience rode took a sharp turn. "I started *Ishmael* that afternoon," he recalled, "the afternoon I kissed off my political future." The controversial work on *Moby-Dick* was finished four months later, "on August 6, 1945, the day Truman bombs Hiroshima."[37]

Ezra Pound was in Washington at St. Elizabeth's Hospital and, as he had done with Dahlberg, Olson introduced himself and became a frequent visitor. Some of his first poems had found impressive outlets: "Lower Field—Enniscorthy" (*Harper's*), "A Lion upon the Floor" (*Harper's Bazaar*), and "Only Red Fox, Only the Crow" (*Atlantic Monthly*). Pound was quite taken with the manuscript of *Call Me Ishmael*. "There's only one bad sentence in your book," he told Olson. Predictably, that sentence was "Now, in spite of the corruption of the myth of fascism, the swing is out and back."[38] Even with Pound's imprimatur, however, the book had some difficulty finding a publisher. Lewis Mumford and F. O. Matthiessen advised Harcourt Brace to reject it, and it was only after Harry Levin and Jay Leyda finally sponsored it at Reynal and Hitchcock that it found, at last, a home.

Its author, Olson, was also seeking some kind of voca-

tional home during the years from 1947 until 1951. He
flirted with academe in an offhand, free-lance sort of way,
lecturing at the University of Washington in Seattle,
American University in Washington, and, in 1947, at Black
Mountain on the invitation of Josef Albers. Eventually he
would serve as Dahlberg's replacement at Black Mountain
when the isolation, the primitive conditions, and the students all proved too much for his former friend. Also
during this time he was tapping his creative energies and
making what proved to be enduring, influential associations. He conceived the plan for the *Maximus Poems* in 1947
and completed "The Kingfishers" in 1949. In his lecture-
journey to the West he had met the anthropologist Carl
Sauer and Robert Duncan, both of whom were to have a
great impact on him. In Washington, D.C., he befriended
the artist Corrado Cagli, who whetted his inchoate interests in non-Euclidean space-time. He even lectured at
the opening of Cagli's exhibit on "Drawings in the 4th Dimension." Almost inevitably this period of intellectual,
creative, and social activity finally percolated into the essay
that was to establish Olson's base as a postmodernist literary theorist, "Projective Verse."

It was Black Mountain College, however, that finally
gave Olson what he sought: the promise of at last ending
the "estrangement," a potential milieu for the "familiar."
Black Mountain College and Charles Olson were waiting
to happen to each other. He came to the college in 1951
directly from Lerma, Campeche, Mexico, where he had
spent six months testing a number of anthropological assumptions among the Mayan ruins and the present-day
Lerma people. The significance of this experience on Olson's life is documented in "The Human Universe," *The
Mayan Letters*, and *Letters to Origin*, and, in retrospect,
nothing else could have been better preparation for his ar-
rival on the Black Mountain campus. He had already, for
example, renewed his hostility to the scholarly establishment, discovering in Mexico how wrong-headed the archeological presuppositions of the funded expeditions had
been in their exploration and interpretation of the ruins:

"It is unbearable what knowledge of the past has been allowed to become, what function of human memory has been dribbled out to in the hands of these learned monsters whom people are led to think 'know'" (*HU*, 12). Perhaps he sensed in the mountains of North Carolina a hint of the "stance" he detected in the Lermas who, although "they are poor failures in the modern world," nevertheless "wear their flesh with that difference which the understanding that it is common leads to.... The admission these people give me and one another is direct, and the individual who peers out from that flesh is precisely himself, is a curious wandering eye like me" (*HU*, 6–7).

At any rate Olson arrived in the summer of 1951 to a college that had begun in a frenzy of eccentric hope but that now had fallen into a serious stage of disintegration. Many of the old faculty had left and new faculty for the fall had yet to be hired. Olson himself had been recruited this time by the enthusiasm of a group of students led by one faculty member, Mary Caroline Richards, who worked very hard to entice him to come. Olson was a kind of last hope and it was inevitable that, given the circumstances, this six-foot-seven, 250-pound mountain of charisma would literally take over. He did, but in a way that drew Black Mountain back to its original roots in the nontraditional, open manner that its founder, John Rice, characterized. Duberman cites some excerpts from an extended faculty meeting, held during the fall and winter of Olson's first year, that was devoted to talking over the school's "educational aims." Olson's contributions to the dialogue are typical:

> Mr. Olson said that this place goes blind, and it is as legitimate to go blind in education as in other areas, meaning you don't make *a priori* definitions of what you intend to accomplish.

> Mr. Olson said that ... BM's type is to take care of the marginal area, the aberrant, which the general area of education does not accommodate....

> Mr. Olson said that . . . the individual is more complex than any curriculum . . . he objected to a theory or chronological order of studies . . . man is different from what we've thought and . . . the principle on which education has been based has to be changed . . . everything is based on things, and knowledge is of no use itself but only in use. . . .

> Mr. Olson said that we gain by the fact that we do not make plans for a curriculum.[39]

Black Mountain, too, was to place its trust in obedience. No a priori definitions, no chronological order, no plans for a curriculum. A blind trust in itself, or perhaps a blind trust in Olson "as the rail." And it worked, at least on Olson's terms. The academic emphasis shifted from the plastic to the writing arts, and the college could eventually claim a distinguished list of its products making influential contributions to the world of letters: Ed Rumacker, John Wieners, Joel Oppenheimer, Ed Dorn, Fielding Dawson, not to mention Jonathan Williams, Robert Creeley, and Robert Duncan, who, while not bona fide "products" of Black Mountain, nevertheless drew from the association.

The *Black Mountain Review*, in 1954, became the house organ of the faithful. Creeley, its editor, describes its significance in this way:

> We did use Olson as a locus without question. We were variously involved with Pound and Williams. . . . We weren't leaning, I think, on Olson's condition, but we were using a premise which he of course had made articulate in projective verse. We were trying to think of how a more active sense of poetry might be got, and that's I think the coincidence we share, or rather the coincident commitment: that each one of us felt that the then existing critical attitudes towards verse, and that the then existing possibilities for publication for general activity in poetry particularly, were extraordinarily narrow.[40]

The *Review* gave focus to what Creeley calls the "premise"

of projective verse in the way *Origin* a few years had show-cased its beginnings. Olson's network of contacts broadened, and it opened the *Review*'s pages to a remarkable number of new talents. The final issue, for example, contained: Allen Ginsberg's "America," Jack Kerouac's "From October in the Railroad Earth," poems by Gary Snyder, Philip Whalen, Michael McClure, a section of William Burrough's then unpublished *Naked Lunch*, and a segment of Hubert Selby's *Last Exit to Brooklyn*.

If there is such a thing as a "golden age" in a man's life, the Black Mountain years were certainly Olson's. He finished the *Maximus Poems* there amid the administrative and pedagogical turmoil, but more than that he was using himself on all fronts, pushing the implications of his "stance" in dance, drama, ceramics, prose, mythology, physics, and mathematics—using himself as well as a forceful impact on others who would never lose his indelible stamp. He was the complete professor of a counter-university nurturing; as Kenner puts it, "antibodies for academicism, from a rogue academy."[41]

But Black Mountain was much more than a rogue academy for Olson. It was the seat of his faith, his "polis," his Eden, from which it was almost inevitable that he should fall. In 1957, while he was superintending the closing and sale of the campus, he mailed this epitaph to his second wife, Betty, which measures the depth of his commitment to the college:

> —all the ultimate Adam of this American place hoped for, was 14, 14 who could take a vow of obedience. "Poverty?", he sd, to the Bishop of Raleigh when the able man noticed the farmhouse needed paint. "I should say. And a form of chastity? Claritas. But the last vow? Who knows, any more, what it is that one does obey to?"
>
> "It was a polis," sd his friend, "no wonder you wanted to take part in its creation."[42]

Some wonder if Olson remained quite the same "ultimate Adam" once he closed that Black Mountain "polis" so suggestively founded on the shore of Lake Eden. Perhaps in retrospect one can detect a fall, or at least a gradual erosion of that peculiar brand of ascetic innocence that Olson possessed. The intense classroom marathons of Black Mountain (often an Olson class might begin in the afternoon, proceed through the night and end the next morning) would later give way to the easy indulgences of the college lecture circuit where student audiences, primed for unkempt mystical insights from an advertised eccentric colossus, all too easily confused unprepared idiosyncrasy for gnomic wisdom. The ambitiously organized course outlines of the Black Mountain days (now published as *The Special View of History*) are supplanted by random recollection and impromptu inspiration. Chad Walsh's account of a Beloit College performance is typical:

> ... I recall no prepared manuscript, and I'm not at all sure he had any notes, though possibly they were on scraps of paper too small to be visible where I was sitting. He gave the impression of someone thinking as he went along. It was as though he were wrestling with some demon of language, trying to put into words the ideas that already existed in preverbal state. Often there would be long pauses. Once he spent several minutes rifling through the chaotic contents of a cloth bag, looking for a short quotation which seemed to be the key to a point he wanted to make.[43]

Kenner feels that "Olson turned incoherence into a style" and succeeded in transforming the poem's context from the page to the campus reading in his later years.[44] It is doubtful that Olson would have quarreled with that. He might even have been pleased, for where but in the participatory atmosphere of a college reading can a poem be more decidedly what Olson insisted it was—act? And as for incoherence as a style, chapter 2 will have much to say on that issue. Nevertheless, one does sense a falling off in Olson after Black Mountain—a kind of homelessness that even Gloucester could not remedy that, despite Olson's fervid convictions about "place," suffuses his work with a sense of rootlessness. Kenner concludes that "a poetry that had patrolled the very limits of coherence commenced indulging itself in cosmic sweep,"[45] and few would seriously argue. In one sense, all of his poems are really cosmologies in disguise; the only thing that changed in the later work was that the disguise was dropped and that the ultimate Adam had finally revealed himself as the ultimate mythologist.

Judgments must wait, however, for the appropriate criteria to be set and the evidence to be examined. What is important now is to savor the nature of the man who so paradoxically was captured while he lived and was retained even after death by the very academic institutions that he charged had "cauterized our nerve ends." For all his incessant clamor against curricula, against systems, schematics, a priori assumptions, here is Olson, revealed in his notes, his drafts, his finished prose pieces as the ultimate schematizer of all. Underneath all the bohemian pretensions, the ascetic individualism, the unconventional life-style is, finally, the professor. And now in death academe reclaims her own. His own "archives" with curator are housed at the University of Connecticut; his own scholarly journal, *Olson*, regularly keeps Olson "scholars" abreast of materials related to the "field"; other scholarly quarterlies have devoted full issues to the man and his work. If the label "academic poet" sits awkwardly on Charles Olson, "academic industry" perhaps does not.

NOTES

1. Martin Duberman, *Black Mountain: An Exploration in Community* (New York: E. P. Dutton, 1972), p. 12.
2. See "On Black Mountain (II)" (transcription of a taped interview of Olson by Andrew S. Leinhoff), *Olson* 8 (Fall 1977): 90: "He [the lawyer for the Corporation of Black Mountain] had, prior to this suit, under a Norman law, made me personally, as rector and chairman of the board by that time point . . . the owner of all of Black Mountain."

3. Reported from an Olson conversation, June 13, 1968, by Ann Charters in *Olson/Melville: A Study in Affinity* (Berkeley, Calif.: Oyez, 1968), p. 84.

4. See Charles Olson, "Introductory Statement for Black Mountain College Catalogue, Spring Semester, 1952," *Olson* 2 (Fall 1974): 25–26.

5. Olson often tends to use the word *feeling* in the technical sense that Whitehead uses the term: "there are two species of prehensions: (a) 'positive prehensions' which are termed 'feelings,' and (b) 'negative prehensions' which are said to 'eliminate from feeling'" (*Process and Reality* [New York: Macmillan Co., 1929], p. 35).

6. Quoted from Keats by Olson as the epigraph to *The Special View of History*, ed. Ann Charters (Berkeley, Calif.: Oyez, 1970), p. 14.

7. Duberman, *Black Mountain*, p. 337.

8. Fielding Dawson, "A Letter from Black Mountain," *Olson* 2 (Fall 1974): 5–6.

9. Charles Boer, *Charles Olson in Connecticut* (Chicago: Swallow Press, 1975), p. 25.

10. Duberman, *Black Mountain*, p. 347.

11. Ibid., p. 369.

12. Edward Dahlberg, *The Confessions of Edward Dahlberg* (New York: George Braziller, 1971), p. 257 passim.

13. Walter Sutton, *American Free Verse: The Modern Revolution in Poetry* (New York: New Directions, 1973), p. 175.

14. James Dickey, *Babel to Byzantium: Poets & Poetry Now* (New York: Farrar, Straus and Giroux, 1968), pp. 137–38.

15. Quoted in Allen Ginsberg, *Allen Verbatim*, ed. Gordon Ball (New York: McGraw-Hill Book Co., 1974), p. 134.

16. Ibid. *Y & X* was a foldover of five poems containing five drawings by Corrado Cagli published by Caresse Crosby's Black Sun Press. The poems are: "The K," "The Green Man," "La Preface," "The Moebius Strip," and "Trinacria."

17. "Songs around the Mountain," *TLS*, 25 November 1965.

18. Charters, *Olson/Melville*, p. 84.

19. Charles Olson, letter to Cid Corman in *The Gist of Origin*, ed. Cid Corman (New York: Grossman Publishers, 1975), p. 500.

20. Charters, *Olson/Melville*, p. 83.

21. Alfred North Whitehead, *Process and Reality* (New York: Macmillan Co., 1929), p. 196.

22. Unpublished lecture entitled "To Make It Clear," contained in the "Institute I" folder in the Charles Olson Archives, University of Connecticut (hereafter referred to by the Library of Congress abbreviation CtU).

23. Robert Bly, "A Wrong Turning in American Poetry," *Choice* 3 (1963): 36.

24. Olson, *The Gist of Origin*, p. 497.

25. In "Equal, That Is, to the Real Itself" Olson sees the impact of the

concept of non-Euclidean space as forcing a new stance toward reality: "[man] was suddenly possesssed or repossessed of a character of being, a thing among things, which I shall call his physicality" (*HU*, 118).

26. Charles Olson, "Journal of Swordfishing Cruise on the Doris M. Hawes," *Olson* 7 (Spring 1977): 24.
27. Ibid., p. 28.
28. A reading list that Olson compiled for Ed Dorn, then a student at Black Mountain preparing for his examination. It has been published separately and in Charles Olson, *Additional Prose*, ed. George F. Butterick (Bolinas, Calif.: Four Seasons Foundation), pp. 3–14.
29. "The first words of his [Herodotus's] book—*oi logoi*—are 'those skilled in the logoi'—not 'historians.' '*Istorin* in him appears to mean 'finding out for oneself,' instead of depending on hearsay. The word had already been used by the philosophers. But while they were looking for truth, Herodotus is looking for the evidence" (*SVH*, p. 20).
30. Boer, *Charles Olson*, p. 17.
31. See Charters, *Olson/Melville*, p. 7.
32. Dahlberg, *Confessions*, p. 257 passim.
33. Boer, *Charles Olson*, p. 18.
34. Charters, *Olson/Melville*, p. 9.
35. Ibid., p. 10.
36. Boer, *Charles Olson*, p. 37.
37. Ibid., p. 38.
38. Charters, *Olson/Melville*, p. 10.
39. Duberman, *Black Mountain*, pp. 340–41.
40. Ibid., p. 390.
41. Hugh Kenner, *A Homemade World: The American Modernist Writers* (New York: Alfred A. Knopf, 1975), p. 176.
42. Charles Olson, "Obit," *Olson* 2 (Fall 1974): 60.
43. See introduction by Charles Olson to *Poetry and Truth*, transcr. and ed. George Butterick (San Francisco: Four Seasons Foundation, 1971), p. 5.
44. Kenner, *Homemade World*, p. 182.
45. Ibid., p. 181.

2

The Grammar of Illiteracy

These Days
whatever you have to say, leave
the roots on, let them
dangle
And the dirt
just to make clear
where they came from
—*Archaeologist of Morning*

Once at a poetry reading at Brandeis Charles Olson "got so damned offended" that he screamed at his audience, "You people are so literate I don't want to read to you anymore." To underscore the seriousness of his point, he added, "It's very crucial today to be sure that you stay illiterate simply because literacy is wholly dangerous, so dangerous that I'm involved everytime I read poetry, in the fact that I'm reading to people who are literate—and they are *not* hearing. They may be listening with all their minds, but they don't hear." [1]

It is hard to hear someone when he is shouting all the time, Cid Corman once observed of Olson, but it is not just the volume, the content, nor the dogmatism of Olson's utterances that dismay even his most sympathetic listeners; it is his conviction—a rigorously practiced one—that language should never surrender the fullness of experience for the sake of logical tidiness.

Capturing the fullness of experience is a creative ambition that can hardly be challenged, but how much untidiness can an audience of listeners or readers tolerate? Chad Walsh, a sympathetic but "literate" listener at an Olson performance at Beloit College, responded to the experience perhaps as many baffled readers have responded to Olson's work at large:

38

Once in a while some brief remark would seem to press a button in my mind and a light would gleam, very briefly. I would seem to have a precious insight, though afterwards I could never recall what it was. Mainly, though, I found myself vainly trying to discover a topic sentence somewhere, or discern the connection of anything to anything.... I suspect that Olson was already living in the world of complex simultaneity, with its own and different rules of logic. (*PT*, 6)

Walsh is considerably more gracious than other detractors who have found Olson's roots-and-all style "pretentious," "more manner than matter," "unspeakably sentimental," and "a rhetoric not easily distinguished from bluff."[2] To such critics Olson's unabashed "illiteracy" is a cultural offense that is pathetically but irresistibly vulnerable to patronizing sneers and elegant put-downs.

Walsh's patient dismay, however, ought perhaps to be gauged against Frank Davey's ardent apology for the same Beloit lecture-reading: "Somebody tries to toss the universe in your lap. You duck. Hell, it's heavy, no handles. But on Olson's side not that easy to throw."[3] Handles (and here Davey surely has in mind topic sentences, connectives, and the other amenities of "literate" grammar) certainly would make the world easier to toss, but would such a domesticated missile, so accommodated with handles, be the one of "complex simultaneity" that Olson experienced? Would not the handles distort the configuration, alter the trajectory? Would not such a universe so equipped become the captive of its own equipage and evolve as a universe of discourse rather than a universe of experience? Such is Olson's position and the basis of his defense of illiteracy.

Both Davey and Walsh seem instinctively to respond to Olson's style in cosmological terms—a *world* of "complex simultaneity," a handleless *universe*—and for very good reasons, because the real underlying issue to their debate goes well beyond literacy, well beyond style, to the very ontological foundations upon which language rests. They are arguing the nature of "being" that language attends. Is that world of "complex simultaneity" without handles the familiar kind of Euclidean reality to which the grammar and syntax of our conventional language has been accommodated, or is it a new conception of "being" so remote from Euclid's orderly universe that it renders traditional expressive structures obsolete? In other words, is reality substantial, discrete, and vulnerable to forces, or is it force itself, a continuous flow of constantly changing energy concentrations much like changes in an electromagnetic field? How do such ontological alternatives affect the conduct and the structure of language?

Olson's position is implicit in the famous opening line of his poem "The Kingfishers":

> What does not change / is the will to change
>
> $(D, 5)$

Not only does this utterance brand him as an unabashed neo-Heraclitean, but it also heralds his growing ontological conviction that a "contrary Renaissance" had occurred in the mid-nineteenth century that had corrected the "error on matter" that, since Aristotle, had kept man "estranged from that with which he is most familiar" $(SVH, 14)$. The initiators of that "contrary Renaissance" were the non-Euclidean mathematicians Bolyai, Lobatschewsky, and ultimately Bernard Riemann, and their work, as Olson was to put it, "redefined the Real" $(HU, 117)$. Having been lured by the Greeks into believing that reality was made of "substance" that possessed "properties" and was passively subject to "causes" of which it became the "effect," we became epistemologically and linguistically estranged from the immediate experience of things. We were, Olson believed, imprisoned in an artificial "universe of discourse" $(HU, 4)$ that the very syntax and grammar of our language seemed to validate.

Riemann, in particular, showed how man could regain his world by developing an alternative to the rigid Euclidean way of regarding the universe. Riemann, Olson explains, "distinguished two kinds of manifold, the discrete (which would be the old system, and it includes discourse, language as it had been since Socrates) and, what he took to be more true, the continuous" (*HU*, 117). The "continuous" conception of reality exposed the Greek "error on matter" by presenting a world characterized by process and change rather than inert substance and properties. Thanks to the non-Euclideans, the world had been liberated from its Greek stranglehold. Man was no longer estranged. "Nothing was now inert fact," Olson chortled,

> all things were there for feeling, to promote it, and be felt; and man, in the midst of it ... was suddenly possessed or repossessed of a character of being, a thing among things, which I shall call his physicality. It made a re-entry of or to the universe. Reality was without interruption, and we are still in the business of finding out how all action, and thought, have to be refounded. (*HU*, 118)

The poem "La Torre" (*AM*) vividly pictures what re-entry to the universe really means by characterizing it as a liberation from a prison of Hellenism. The tower itself is constructed of Greek epistemological presuppositions in which "the head" and the "the hands" are established as distinctions that separate man from the universe surrounding his stony bastion. He is defined as a rational animal (the head) and a maker (the hands). By virtue of these superior attributes he manipulates Nature for his purposes and exiles himself from Her. His tower is testament to his denial that he is a "thing among things." It is Hellenism itself and it effectively dramatizes how Greek tradition has "estranged us from that with which we are most familiar."

But the tower is also language. It is a Babel of architectural rigidity that blocks out light. Its destruction necessitates a grammatical reconstruction:

> To begin again, Lightning
> is an axe, transfer
> of force subject to object is
> order: destroy!

Olson's phrasings here are virtually lifted from Fenollosa's *The Chinese Written Character as a Medium for Poetry*,"[4] and that essay's attack on the artificiality of "the sentence" as a "complete thought" helps us to appreciate the full measure of Olson's call for a linguistic "re-entry to the universe." Fenollosa's position is simple. "Nature herself has no grammar," he argues, and so the classical grammarians' definition of the sentence as "a complete thought" or as a construction "uniting subject and predicate" is simply at odds with reality. There is no completeness in Nature and therefore there should be no completeness in the sentence. The notion of subject and predicate forces an unnatural subjectivity onto man's relationship with his universe. The sentence requires that he view himself as an "I" that does something to an "it." Thus, concludes Fenollosa, "The sentence . . . is not an attribute of nature but an accident of man as a conversational animal."

In place of the syntactically defined sentence Fenollosa would have a *"transference of power . . .* a flash of lightning."[5] In other words, the sentence is not grammar; it is power.

The destruction of the tower means the destruction of the sentence, but it also has a physical effect on man. It causes his "jaws to grind" and his nostrils [to] flare / to let the breath in."A linguistic complement to "discourse" enters—speech. What had been in the tower a "universe of discourse" (*HU*, 4) now becomes a language that accommodates both "discourse" *and* speech. "La Torre" poetically renders what Olson argues in the "Human Universe":

> We have lived long in a generalizing time, at least since 450 B.C.. And it has had its effects on the best of men, on the best of things. Logos, or discourse, for example, has, in that time, so worked its abstractions into our concept and use of language that language's other function, speech, seems . . . in need of restoration. (*HU*, 3–4)

Speech is the linguistic mode of physicality, just as "discourse" is the mode of the mind. When breath links them together, a new epistemological foundation for man results. He is no longer locked in a tower to which his five senses condemn him; he now experiences an openness to the world that his body affords him. "Physicality," we recall, is a bodily "depth sensibility" (*AP*, 17) that is tantamount to what Olson's favorite metaphysician, Alfred North Whitehead, calls "causal efficacy."[6] The essence of the idea is that the body, as distinct from the five senses, is itself an epistemological instrument. It "feels" reality in addition to the sense perceptions that the five senses supply. Olson's recurring stress on the vital importance of breath stems from a conviction that breath liberates the "self" from its traditional seat in the mind and reestablishes it in its proper place—the body. Thus, our knowledge of the world and our expression of that knowledge through speech comes from inside us. "One's life," says Olson, "is informed from and by one's own literal body, . . . the intermediary, the intervening thing, the interruptor, the resistor. The self" (*AP*, 18).

The fall of the tower naturally precipitates a sense of vulnerability, for

> Where there are no walls
> there are no laws, forms, sounds, odors
> to grab hold of

It takes a while to adjust to freedom and accept the challenge that Olson poses in this poem and in the "Human Universe" as well:

> We stay unaware how two means of discourse the Greeks appear to have invented hugely intermit our participation in our experience, and so prevent discovery. They are what followed from Socrates' readiness to generalize, his willingness . . . to make a "universe" out of discourse instead of letting it rest in its most serviceable place. (It is not sufficiently observed that logos, and the reason necessary to it, are only a stage which a man must master and not what they are taken to be, final discipline. Beyond them is direct perception and the con-

traries which dispose of argument. The harmony of the
universe, and I include man, is not logical, or better, is
post-logical, as is the order of any created thing.) With
Aristotle, the two great means appear: logic and classification. And it is they that have so fastened themselves
on habits of thought that action is interfered with, absolutely interfered with, I should say. (*HU*, 4)

The toppling of the walls (and with them "laws, forms,
sounds, odors") literally creates an open space where
"FORM IS NEVER MORE THAN AN EXTENSION OF
CONTENT" (*HU*, 52):

> Let the tower fall!
> Where space is born
> man has a beach to ground on
> > (*AM*)

The overriding intent of "La Torre," then, is to celebrate man's reconciliation with his immediate experience—to end his estrangement from "that with which he is
most familiar." To accomplish the reconciliation, Olson
believed that "particularism has to be fought for anew"
(*HU*, 4) and "La Torre" demonstrates the strategy vividly:

> We have taken too little note of this:
> the sound of a hammer on a nail can be as clear as
> the blood a knife can make spurt from a round taut
> > belly

These pure, immediate acts that the passage documents—creation, ritual and death—are particulars that
must be fought for with weapons that are not likely to be
found in the tower. Different tools and materials are required, and as Olson has us stand grounded on the beach
he directs our attention out to the sea where

> rafts come towards us lashed of wreckage and young
> > tree.
> They bring the quarried stuff we need to try this new
> > found strength.

> It will take a new stone, new tufa, to finish off this
> rising tower.

The "new tufa" of which the new tower will be made will
be the stone of the Mayan glyphs that so excited Olson's
imagination in Campeche—glyphs that on their "very
face" are "verse" with the signs "so clearly and densely chosen that, cut in stone, they retain the power of the objects
of which they are images" (*HU*, 7).

Particularism and *physicality* are just two of the terms that
Olson uses to suggest the configuration of the new tower.
Topos, place, objectism, complementarity, and, of course, *projective* all address that stance which Olson insists will return
man's universe to him and render him once again privy to
the "secrets objects share" (*HU*, 60). The perspective from
the old tower sees this as illiteracy; after all, denizens of the
old tower are accustomed to a discrete rather than a continuous world. They prefer their discourse to be repre-
sentational and mimetic and therefore invariably "referential to reality" (*HU*, 96). The grammar of literacy, as
Olson sees it, fails because it is merely *about* experience.
The grammar of illiteracy succeeds because it is *of* it. "If
anybody wants forever never to enjoy language," Olson
once counseled (resolutely practicing what he preached),
"they will remember grammar as it was taught from those
abhorrent Alexandrians down to probably every poor
school kid right now."[7]

But in a very practical sense, what is it about Alexandrian grammar and the "universe of discourse" that is so
abhorrent to Olson? Has not its generalizing capability, in
spite of its subversion of the "familiar," actually served
both western science and humanism rather handsomely
since Aristotle? Does it really make any practical difference
if a disparity exists between language and the ontology
that underlies it? If man's thoughts, feelings and com-
mands are reasonably well served by "discourse"—if our
language "works"—is it not impractical, no matter what
theoretical sense it might make, to "refound" it upon
another basis?

Olson's reply would be that "discourse" has nothing to do with humanism; in fact, it is humanism's antithesis. Not only does it estrange man from that which is most familiar, it creates a new universe in which he has no part. It accords science, for instance, an autonomous, humanly *un*related existence, ignoring the fact that reality is never more than "as much nature as man is engaged with."[8] In other words, "discourse" artificially inflates reality by extending it beyond human limits, and for this reason Olson vigorously contends that Art is a much superior epistemological tool than Science:

> The flopping around, in whatever order, of the galaxies and that infinite out beyond, now that it's home, in light, and signals and mass points are the best narration physics can manage. Men say Hoogh to that Honey. . . . This is no knowledge superior to an arts action when it is superior.[9]

What he means is that once we acknowledge that we live in a "human universe" with boundaries set in terms of "as much nature as man is engaged with," then Art is a more appropriate tool than Science simply because it respects the built-in limits of humanism—that it is human. The seat of reality is in the human physiology:

> It's a matter of where the music and the color and the words are. They are in the body and the motion and that's where they and the real become one, in the passings and intersections of a physicality which talks and runs and wears what it does.[10]

Illiteracy, or to use its more respectable name, the "projective," is no mere peevish kicking of syntax in the teeth to spite Aristotle; it is a humanist attempt to subvert the inhuman rigidities and inflations of reality that lie embedded in classical "humanism" itself. The specific rigidities and inflations it seeks to purge are: forms, classes, ideals, conventions, similes, symbols, allegories, comparisons, and descriptions—all things, in short, that betray "particularism" by remaining *referential* rather than *of* reality. Again, "FORM IS NEVER MORE THAN AN EXTENSION OF CONTENT."

"Projective Verse," which first appeared in *Poetry New York* in 1950, was Olson's first public defense of the grammar of illiteracy. This essay was probably what Hugh Kenner had in mind when he observed that "if Olson's expositions seem messy, it is because they are less composed than talked about."[11] In a broad sense, the grammar of illiteracy is the grammar of talk, and "Projective Verse" is Olson talking—talking rapid-fire, urgently, and with more concern for the act of his *own* engagement with his material than with his comprehensibility to a general audience. It is full of "difficulties" and "proper confusions" that are not limited to the infamous violations of "correct usage and form" that Olson's critics wince at with regularity. The essay *assumes* rather than creates its context. The uninitiated reader feels as though he is entering an ongoing conversation late after the terminology has been established and the issues already defined. A blurb on Olson's style from *The Floating Bear* says it all: "Solid, declamatory prose, though he, like Pound, expects you to know his subject as well as he does. Many times like notes to himself, you are infuriated that you don't know what he's talking about because you didn't read a certain book."[12]

Olson's enormous and diverse reading, combined with the fact that he "reads to write,"[13] virtually assures many bewildered and infuriated critics. With little contextual assistance from Olson, and thus thrown on their own resources, these critics understandably assume their own contexts for "Projective Verse," which are usually much, much narrower than Olson's, and which inevitably confine his dogmas exclusively to the Pound-Williams objectivist axis. The result is usually a plausible critique of a misleadingly "reduced" Olson.

Some examples: "What Olson's notion of 'open' verse does is simply to provide creative irresponsibility with the semblance of a rationale which may be defended in heated and cloudy terms by its supposed practitioners" (James

Dickey);[14] "'Projective Verse,' ... though it has been very influential, it would not be unfair to describe as the worst prose published since *Democratic Vistas*. ... 'Put down anything so long as you keep writing' would be a fair enough paraphrase" (Thom Gunn);[15] "Olson consistently insinuates ... that his theory of poetry is revolutionary. Yet his main deviation from the Pound-Williams aesthetic is that he muddles their concepts" (Marjorie Perloff).[16] On the other hand, Williams himself wrote to Robert Creeley after reading the essay, "I share your excitement, it is as if the whole area lifted. It's the sort of thing we are after and must have."[17]

The problem is that Olson regarded "Projective Verse" as merely the literary tip of a metaphysical iceberg. His detractors tended to see it as an autonomous poetics. Consequently, Olson's dogmas, some new, many borrowed, seem derivative rather than revolutionary when they are extracted from their larger context. Consider dogma one, for example:

> (1) the *kinetics* of the thing. A poem is energy transferred from where the poet got it ... by way of the poem itself to ... the reader. ... Then the poem itself must, at all points, be a high energy-construct and, at all points, an energy-discharge. (*HU*, 52)

Certainly this is little more than Fenollosa's concept of the sentence as a "transference of power" applied to verse. Defining the poem as an "energy-construct" is hardly innovative either; Williams and Pound had been saying as much for years. But the intensity with which Olson urges the perhaps tired dogma overwhelms an important qualification that follows it and that at least suggests a philosophical depth to Olson's version relatively absent in Pound and Williams:

> From the moment he ventures into FIELD COMPOSITION—puts himself in the open—he can go by no track other than the one the poem under hand declares, for itself. Thus he has to behave, and be, instant by instant,

aware of some several forces just now beginning to be examined. (*HU*, 52)

This is less poetics than epistemological position and when it is viewed against the context of Olson's complete "stance towards reality," it reveals inchoate hints of the influence of Whitehead, Jung, and even Merleau-Ponty to come. In other words, the dogma can be seen as merely the poetic facet of the larger philosophy of obedience that so significantly informs Olson's work as a whole.

Dogma number two similarly emerges from an underlying epistemology:

(2)... the *principle*,... FORM IS NEVER MORE THAN AN EXTENSION OF CONTENT (*HU*, 52)

As a principle of poetics, this statement yields little more than the commonplace notion that subject matter should be allowed to discover its own natural form, but again, from the perspective of Olson's comprehensive stance, it involves the status of a man (be he poet or not) in relation to his environment. Man should resist imposing his forms egotistically upon Nature as a matter of perceptual propriety. The very urge to impose form upon Nature creates "lyrical interference" (*HU*, 59) both in poetry and life.

Dogma three reads:

(3) the *process* of the thing, how the principle can be made so to shape the energies that the form is accomplished.... ONE PERCEPTION MUST IMMEDIATELY AND DIRECTLY LEAD TO A FURTHER PERCEPTION. (*HU*, 52)

Here we see once again the poetical application of an ontological truth. If reality, as Riemann and Olson both believed, is a continuous rather than a discrete manifold, the expression of that reality accordingly should be continuous and not discrete. Thus the dogma proposes a poetic process consonant with the natural process of the universe. Olson's notion here is somewhat less naive than Thom

Gunn's characterization of it: "Put down anything so long as you keep writing."

The genuine originality of "Projective Verse" cannot be appreciated from the dogmas, which, like gaudy blossoms, inevitably steal the show, but must be savored at the roots that lie deep in the soil of an alternative humanism. In "Projective Verse" this alternative humanism is dubbed "objectism." Olson is obviously nervous about that term and goes to some lengths (vainly, as it turns out[18]) to distinguish it from the "objectivism" of Pound and Williams. He defines it as

> a word to be taken to stand for the kind of relation of man to experience which a poet might state as the necessity of a line or a work to be as wood is, to be as clean as wood is as it issues from the hand of nature, to be as shaped as wood can be when a man has had his hand to it. Objectism is the getting rid of the lyrical interference of the individual as ego, of the "subject" and his soul, that peculiar presumption by which western man has interposed himself between what he is as a creature of nature (with certain instructions to carry out) and those other creations of nature which we may, with no derogation, call objects. For a man is himself an object, whatever he may take to be his advantages, particularly at that moment that he achieves an humilitas sufficient to make him of use. (*HU*, 59–60)

That this definition can be taken as "merely Pound's 'objectivism'" in not very new dress, as Marjorie Perloff does,[19] is a good example of how easy it is for the parochial literary mind to bend all to its own presuppositions. Perloff backs up her assertion with Pound's famous remark from "Retrospect": "I believe that the proper and perfect symbol is the natural object, that if a man use 'symbols' he must use them so that their symbolic function does not obtrude." Undoubtedly, Olson's analogy of poetic creation to wood draws Perloff's charge, but the fact is that Olson isn't talking about symbols here nor is he even talking about perception; he is simply once again outlining that epistemological posture that he ubiquitously calls the proper "stance towards reality." "It comes to this," he continues,

> the use of a man, by himself and thus by others, lies in how he conceives his relation to nature, that force to which he owes his somewhat small existence. If he sprawl, he shall find little to sing but himself, . . . But if he stays inside himself, if he is contained within his nature as he is participant in the larger force, he will be able to listen, and his hearing through himself will give him secrets objects share. (*HU*, 69)

In a letter to Creeley, he comes at "objectism" from a slightly different but more succinct direction:

> man as object in field of force declaring self as force because is force in exactly such relation & can accomplish expression of self as force by conjecture, & displacement in a context best, now, seen as space more than a time such:
> which I take it, is precise contrary to, what we have had, as "humanism," with, man, out of all proportion of, relations, thus, so mis-centered, becomes, dependent on, only, a whole series of "human" references which, so made, make only anthropomorphism, and thus, make a mush of, *any* reality, conspicuously, his own, not to speak of, how all other forces (ticks, water-lilies, or snails) become only descriptive objects. (*ML*, 67)

Obviously "objectism" is no mere literary bias; it is a way of life. It is *humilitas*, a rejection of the "Egotistical Sublime," a denial of the subject-object predication of Alexandrian grammar and Western epistemology, a "contrary Renaissance," and a useful creative attitude. Why useful? Because when it is employed as "the artist's act in the larger field of objects, [it] leads to dimensions larger than the man" (*HU*, 60).

Those dogmatic blossoms of "Projective Verse" (the "*kinetics* . . . the *principle* . . . the *process* of the thing") are vulnerable to the worst kind of *reductio ad ordinarium* when they are lopped from the plant that nourishes them. The same is true of other corollary points. Olson's comments on "breath," for example: "the line comes (I swear it) from the breath, from the breathing of the man who writes, at the moment he writes . . . for only he, the man who writes, can declare, at every moment, the line, its metric and its ending where its breathing shall come to termination" (*HU*, 54).

A poem that is act itself, not thought about act, is beholden to that authority that issues through the breath from where "all act springs" (*HU*, 61); that is, the physiology of the poet. Lest one think this a mere "heated and cloudy" theory rather than practical methodology, note the results of the experiments of Marcia and Philip Lieberman.[20] The Liebermans compared the "breath-grouping" of Olson's reading of his own poems with those of Keats. They discovered that the distinctiveness of Olson's poems was that they used "breath-groups to delimit and emphasize lines in violation of grammatical restraints." In the Keats poems, on the other hand, breath-groups tended to play a "syntactical role." In total fidelity to his assertions in "Projective Verse," Olson seems to permit the rival delimiting authorities, syntax and breath, to coexist in his poems, which has the effect of breaking down the rigid tyranny of the "logical" sentence and allowing an expansive breath-group flexibility continually to offer interpretive alternatives. In other words, the Liebermans empirically demonstrate that Olson's own poetry in fact does restore "speech-force'" to the language. Breath demonstrably "rights the balance" by asserting its partnership with syntax. Commenting upon their findings from an oral reading of "Maximus, at the Harbor," they ask that we "note that the logical—that is, syntactical—function of the breath-group is still manifested in this reading, even though individual lines are then set apart by individual breath-groups. The disturbance of the listener's expectations that occurs when a breath-group terminates a line in violation of syntactic constraints gives emphasis to the line. The listener has to attend more closely to the line to reach a semantic interpretation."

The "projective" poet, Olson maintained, was one who "manages to register both the acquisitions of his ear *and* the pressures of his breath" (*HU*, 53). In terms of his "stance toward reality," this complementarity of breath and ear is the poetic counterpart to the principle of "physicality," that is, bodily depth sensibility, the notion of the "body-subject." The ear, Olson insists, "is so close to the mind that it is the mind's" (*HU*, 54), just as the breath is so obviously of the body. From the "union of the mind and the ear . . . the syllable is born" (*HU*, 54), Olson tells us, and accordingly, "the line comes (I swear it) from the breath" (*HU*, 54). The poem therefore becomes the uniting act of mind and body achieved through the creative coalition of ear and breath as they spontaneously merge syllable into line. Hence, Olson's much-maligned formula:

the HEAD, by way of the EAR, to the SYLLABLE
the HEART, by way of the BREATH, to the LINE
(*HU*, 55)

Breath, as Olson means it, then, is the instrument of the larger stance towards reality that he has identified as "physicality," but it also serves as means for restoring "speech" to discourse: "breath allows *all* the speech-force of language back in (speech is the 'solid' of verse, is the secret of the poem's energy), because, now, a poem has, by speech, solidity, everything in it can be treated as solids, objects, things" (*HU*, 56). Breath reifies experience by creating an awareness of bodily "depth sensibility" that assures its being felt in addition to its being observed, but it also, Olson claims, reifies the elements of verse. This certainly sounds like standard Objectivist logic: "No ideas but in things" (Williams); "The World must be measured by the eye" (Stevens); "the rock crystal thing" (Marianne Moore); but the difference in Olson's "objectism" is breath. Breath shifts the basis of objectivist reification from perception to physical "depth sensibility" and this is why Olson insists that his position be called "objectism." "Objectism" is no perceptual attitude toward things; it is a comprehensive stance that man assumes toward the world that deliberately humiliates his epistemological status by insisting that he be merely a "thing among things." It is, Olson explains, "the getting rid of the lyrical interference of the individual as ego, of the 'subject" and his soul, that peculiar presumption by which western man has interposed himself between what he is as a creature of nature and those other creations of nature which we may with no derogation, call objects" (*HU*, 59–60).

In a very real sense, then, breath liberates the self from the mind (or soul) and places it physically in the body so that our knowing of the world, our experience and discovery, comes from "inside us/ & at the same time does not feel literally identical with our own physical or mortal self" (*AP*, 17). In other words, "one's life is informed from and by one's own literal body, . . . the intermediary, the intervening thing, the interruptor, the resistor. The self" (*AP*, 18).

From the point of view of one who considers the poet a "maker" or craftsman of "discrete" poems that thereupon become available for analysis, interpretation, and criticism, projective verse will inevitably seem perverse, for it rejects the overt manipulation of reality that such words as "craft" and "art" imply. Fealty to the real is the overriding criterion. Time and again, Olson and his disciples allude to Werner Heisenberg's "uncertainty principle" as a kind of scientific rationale for avoiding artifice, pointing out that just as the instruments of observation in physics distort the reality of the observed phenomenon (we must "freeze" mass to weigh it, and mass is actually never in repose), so in verse the intrusion of literary "devices" artifically stops the ongoing process of "continuous" reality. In short, the "projective" mode asks the poet to assume an attitude of passive obedience to the inner and outer experiences that he registers.

Perhaps the greatest burden of patience falls on the readers of projective literature, for they, even more than the projective writer (who at least has the guidance of his own experiences to assist him) are truly "naked" in the open field. They are advised that a projective poem is a reenactment rather than an artifact and that they should concern themselves with absorbing the energies (rather than substance) that are "held" in a kind of dynamic tension within the field of the poem. The images of the poem, by virtue of the solidity that breath gives them, are allowed the free play of their individual energies, they are advised, even while, through juxtaposition with other images, they create an energy field. The character of the engagement that readers are expected to have is radically different from what they are accustomed to. They are asked to "avoid all irritable reaching after fact and reason" and to remain "in the absolute condition of present things" (*HU*, 118)—that is, in the poem itself.

And yet, is this projective nakedness in the open field, this remaining "in the absolute condition of present things" all that unfamiliar? So many times Olson's art is characterized as mere conversation—Olson talking—and there is more than just a ring of truth to such observations. Talk *is* the template of Olson's style and it is talk that links his style to its underlying ontology. Talk, as opposed to frozen discourse, is spontaneous, ongoing, irreversible, verbal act. The flexibility of conversational talk—its toleration of inconsistencies and logical imprecision—makes it an effective net for gathering particulars even though this advantage may be bought at the expense of vagueness. But what of vagueness? Must it necessarily be a liability? May it not in fact be the only possible mode of expressing "direct perception and the contraries that dispose of argument" that, Olson insists, are "post-logical" and beyond "the irritable reaching after fact and reason" (*HU*, 4)?

Interestingly, the structure of nonwestern languages bears striking resemblance to English informal conversation. By way of accounting for a pervasive, annoying vagueness in the work of the Chinese philosopher Mencius he was attempting to translate, I. A. Richards was struck by how similar that "vagueness" seemed to

the successive attempts that a speaker will sometimes make to convey a thought which does not fit any ready formulation. He may intimate as he switches (with an "or rather" or a "perhaps I ought to say") over from one statement to another, that he is "developing" his thought. Those with a taste for clear, precise views (itself a result of special training) will accuse him of not knowing what he wants to say, or of having really no thought yet to utter. But there is another possibility— that a thought is present whose structure and content are not suited to available formulations, that these successive, perhaps incompatible, statements partly represent, partly misrepresent, an idea independent of them which none the less has its own order and coherent reference.[21]

Is what Richards describes really much different from projective "open" form? Both are unusually supple modes that are immediately reflexive to the "condition of present things." Both function admirably "in uncertainties, Mysteries, doubts, without any irritable reaching after fact and reason." Can it be that the aggravation some feel toward projective verse is simply that it embarrasses them with the fact that our most meaningful experiences occur not in lofty elegies, majestic odes or symmetrical sonnets but in the halting, inconsistent, difficulties and proper confusions of you and I in urgent talk?[22]

Can we, though, seriously regard "you and I in urgent talk" as Art? What happens in talk? Is it a mimetic activity? Does it hold up a mirror to Nature, as Plato insisted Art does? Or, if that claim seems irrelevant, can we hold that talk "improves" on Nature, idealizes it? Obviously, none of the classical approaches touch even near the actuality of Olson's enterprises, for they are mesmerized by the metaphor of artist-as-maker and Art as the-object-made. Talk, however, is an activity, a process, an event. True, it can be notated on a printed page, but its essential value is its movement. Its shifts, its false starts, its indecisions, its non sequiturs—Olson's intensified stammerings, juxtaposings, indirect guesses—these are participatory events that rise to Art when, through heightened intensity and sense of collective experience, they become the requickening of a previous or anticipated emotion through rite, what the Greeks called *dromenon*, "the thing done."[23]

It is the "doing," the acting, that sets the value to Olson's "talk." As Olson's favorite mythologist, Jane Harrison, explains it,

> The Greeks had realized that to perform a rite you must *do* something, that is, you must not only feel something but express it in action, or, to put it psychologically, you must not only receive an impulse, you must react to it.[24]

This kind of "doing" applies not only to the poet but to the reader as well. Talk is a social, collective activity. We may only nod our head occasionally, widen our eyes in surprise, grimace in exasperation or simply sigh, but we are called upon to "do," to react, to engage our energies with those of the poem in urgent conversation.

One final dimension of Olson's "illiteracy" ought to be savored if for no other reason than to appreciate how comprehensively the poet applies and translates his notion of the projective to the whole front of reality. It is his willingness to expose writing to the same ontological challenge that has faced mathematics and physics—that is, how to make it "Equal, That Is, to the Real Itself" (*HU*, 117–22).

That last phrase is the title of Olson's important review-essay of Milton Stern's *The Fine Hammered Steel of Herman Melville* in which Olson spells out in remarkable detail, although in the confusing technical jargon of space-age physics, how he regards projective writing as an inevitable consequence of the same non-Euclidean "redefinition of the Real" (*HU*, 117) that gave birth to relativity theory, quantum physics, and the whole conception of a continuous, as opposed to a classically discrete, universe. This new ontological premise excited Olson because he saw it as a reaffirmation of Heraclitus's view of reality: "All things flow."

"Equal, That Is, to the Real Itself" is a difficult essay partly because so much of it is eclectically wrenched from an unacknowledged source text, Hermann Weyl's *The Philosophy of Mathematics and Natural Science*,[25] and partly because it undertakes to talk of fundamental literary problems in an unfamiliar idiom and from an unfamiliar perspective. Still, it affords perhaps the most mature, most sophisticated rendering of the "stance towards reality" and its impact upon "literacy" that Olson leaves us. The essential argument is that adjustments have to be made to the way in which we "know and present the real" (writing) in order for it to "equal" a continuous rather than a discrete reality. The first obstacle to effecting these adjustments is the "error on matter" that previously was the means by which "one can avoid the real." In a discrete universe the norm for evaluating experience is inert matter. Things are regarded as constant and autonomous, sufficiently so that they are perceived as "substance" that possesses classifiable "qualities." In a continuous universe, however, time, as a fourth dimension, forces us to perceive things no longer as inert "substances," but as "events"—"All things flow." Consequently, projective writing characteristically eschews "qualities" (it is rarely descriptive) and stresses instead the intensive "quantities" of things; that is, their "velocity, force and field strength" within the continuous manifold.

An apt metaphor for such a continuous reality is the electromagnetic field in which interrelated transformations of energy points take place. In such a field discrete formulations, such as subject-object, cause-effect, and even mind-body, give way to the notion of flexible interplay between "things among things." Indeed, Olson eventually underscores this "field" assumption at the end of his essay by a quotation from the mathematician Bernard Riemann, which he assesses as the most "relevant single fact to the experience of *Moby-Dick* and its writer":

> The inertial structure of the world is a real thing which not only exerts effects upon matter but in turn suffers such effects.[26]

What Riemann documents here is a shift from the mechanical view of the world's processes to an organic one.

If the world's structure is "give-and-take"—both exerting and suffering effects—this means that matter itself can no longer be considered inflexibly inert; it too gives and takes. The old Euclidean view of a reality in which inert particles of matter are passively pushed about by arbitrary forces is replaced by the more appropriate notion of fluid interplay. Once again, "All things flow."

But perhaps the most important adjustment projective writing strives for has to do with measurement, for "art is measure" (*HU*, 122). Olson quotes Riemann's corollary to the previous statement on the inertial structure of the world, showing how it affects measurement as well:

> ...the metrical structure of the world is so intimately connected to the inertial structure that the metrical field ... will of necessity become flexible ... the moment the inertial field itself is flexible. (*HU*, 122)

Euclidean measuring techniques are obsolete in a continuous reality because they depend upon the assumption that rigid bodies can move freely in space in order to determine congruence. "What is measure," Olson asks, "when the universe flips and no part is discrete from another part except by the flow of creation itself, in and out, intensive where before it seemed qualitative" (*HU*, 119)? The constant transformations of the continuum cannot be artificially halted to accommodate a yardstick. Reality, Olson concludes, is "a pumping of the real so constant art had to invent measure anew" (*HU*, 119).

Of course the problem of a new measurement was not merely art's, but the problem of all mathematics and science. The unassailable organic integrity of sheer process, which characterizes the continuous manifold, is simply inaccessible to "additive" measurement. As Riemann himself puts it, "for a discrete manifold the principle of measurement is already contained in the concept of this manifold, but for a continuous one it must come from elsewhere."[27]

The "elsewhere" for Olson was "the new world of atomism" that, he claimed, "offered a metrical means as well as a topos different from the discrete" (*HU*, 120).

That means was "congruence," but not the congruence "which had been the measure of space a solid fills in two of its positions" (Euclidean congruence), but a "point-by-point mapping power of such flexibility that anything which stays the same, no matter where it goes and into whatever varying conditions (it can suffer deformation), it can be followed, and, if it is art, led" (*HU*, 120). This non-Euclidean (topological) definition of congruence made it possible to effect the measurement of things in motion, things undergoing the normal transformations characteristic of the continuous manifold. It demanded no reference to metrical absolutes "outside" the continuum or, for that matter, outside the thing itself.

Instead of depending upon a principle of free mobility of rigid bodies in space, topological congruence concerned itself with "automorphic transformations," that is, a "one-to-one mapping $p \rightarrow p'$ of the point field into itself which leaves the basic relations undisturbed."[28] In short, what determines congruence is not similarity of metrical lengths but simple connectedness. The object in the process of transformation within the continuous manifold carries its own congruency standard with it; its point field can be mapped continuously and will always maintain the single invariance of connectedness so long as it does not violate the continuum. As one topologist describes the rules of this form of congruence,

> Arbitrary deformations of curves, surfaces and figures are allowed as long as connectivity is maintained. Therefore, distortion, bending, battering, etc., is allowed, but tearing, cutting, breaking, joining or sticking together, welding, cementing, disregarding of holes, etc., is forbidden. In this type of geometry square and circle, cuboid and sphere are equivalent.[29]

All fine and good. But how does all this affect the projective mode? "Taking it in towards writing," Olson explains,

> the discrete, for example, wasn't any longer a good enough base for discourse: classification was exposed as

mere taxonomy; and logic (and the sentence poised on it, a completed thought, instead of what it has become, an exchange of force) was as loose and inaccurate a system as the body and soul had been, divided from each other and rattling, sticks in a stiff box. (*HU*, 119)

Classification, logic, separation of body and soul, and the "complete" sentence are rejected from the projective on the basis of their ontological inconsistency with *continuous* reality; each, in its way, interrupts the connectedness of the transformational process of the field.

Olson calls such interruptions of connectedness "discontinuous jumps." In writing these jumps take the form of allegories, symbols, comparisons and all other devices that take us out of the continuum altogether or disturb our equality with it. Citing the prose in *Moby-Dick* as an example, Olson points out that Melville

was not tempted . . . to inflate the physical: take the model for the house, the house for the model, . . . using such sets as the mirror image . . . . he was essentially incapable of either allegory or symbol for the best of congruent reason, mirror and model are each figures in Euclidean space, and they are *not* congruent. (*HU*, 121)

Mirror and model (allegory and symbol) are *not* automorphic mappings of their originals; therefore, they violate the topological invariance of connectedness. They are "tears" or "cuts" in the narrative continuum. But more than that, they also violate the epistemological stance that "objectism" dictates by promoting, rather than suppressing, the "lyrical interference of the ego." For example, Melville, according to Olson, "couldn't abuse object as symbol does by depreciating it in favor of subject. Or let image lose its relational force by transferring its occurrence as allegory does. He was already aware of the complementarity of each of two pairs of how we know and present the real—image & object, and action & subject" (*HU*, 121). By forcing a subjective significance on images and objects, symbol and allegory demean their "self-incidence" and artificially elevate the human ego to an uncomely status above other objects.

The grammar of illiteracy, then, is really the grammar of life—life in all its ongoing continuity and unremitting process. It is a grammar that forbids "sprawl," forbids existence outside the "human universe." But for all that, it is a grammar committed to man's physical being, dictated by the heart's "pumping" of the real and, most of all, by the breath that has its beginning in that place from where "all act springs."

NOTES

1. Charles Olson, "Under the Mushroom: The Gratwick Highlands Tape," *Olson* 3 (Spring 1975): 43.
2. See, for example, Roy Fuller, *Owls and Artificers* (London: Andre Deutsch, 1971), pp. 38, 39, 58, 64; James Dickey, *Babel to Byzantium: Poets & Poetry Now* (New York: Farrar, Straus and Giroux, 1968), pp. 136–39; Marjorie Perloff, "Charles Olson and the 'Inferior Predecessors': 'Projective Verse' Revisited," *ELH* 40 (Summer 1973): 285–306.
3. Frank Davey, "Poetry and Truth: The Beloit Lectures and Poems," *Boundary 2* 2, (Fall/Winter 1973–74): 24.
4. Ernest Fenollosa, *The Chinese Written Character as a Medium for Poetry*, ed. Ezra Pound (San Francisco: City Lights Books, 1936). In an unpublished essay, "A New Short Ars Poetica . . ." (*CtU*), Olson writes of Fenollosa, "He changed everything when he said a sentence is by nature."
5. Fenollosa, *Chinese Written Character*, p. 12.
6. Alfred North Whitehead, *Process and Reality* (New York: Macmillan Co., 1919), pp. 255–79.
7. Olson, "A New Short Ars Poetica . . ." (*CtU*).
8. Olson, "Language Is a Thumb' (*CtU*).
9. Ibid.
10. Ibid.
11. Hugh Kenner, *A Homemade World: The American Modernist Writers* (New York: Alfred A. Knopf, 1975), p. 176.
12. *Floating Bear* 30 (November 1964): 98.
13. Olson shared this attribute with his literary hero, Melville, of whom he wrote in *Call Me Ishmael*: "Melville's reading is a gauge of him, at all points of his life. He was a skald, and knew how to appropriate the work of others. He read to write" ([New York: Reynal Hitchcock, 1974], p. 36).
14. Dickey, *Babel to Byzantium*, pp. 137–38.

15. Thom Gunn, "New Books in Review," *The Yale Review* 50 (Summer 1961): 596.

16. Marjorie Perloff, "Charles Olson and the 'Inferior Predecessors': 'Projective Verse' Revisited," *ELH* 40 (Summer 1973): 291.

17. Cited by Robert Creeley in his introduction to *Selected Writings of Charles Olson*, ed. Robert Creeley (New York: New Directions, 1966), p. 6.

18. Despite the attempts of hostile critics to blur Olson's distinction between "objectivism" and "objectism," his point seems clear and well taken to me: "It is no accident that Pound and Williams both were involved variously in a movement which got called 'objectivism.' But that word was then used in some sort of necessary quarrel, I take it, with 'subjectivism.' . . . What seems to me a more valid formulation for present use is 'objectism,' a word taken to stand for the kind of relation of man to experience which a poet might state as the necessity of a line or a work to be as wood is . . . as it issues from the hand of nature." (*HU*, 59). Olson's point goes well beyond perception to epistemological stance, and that is why he is unsatisfied with the word *objectivism*.

19. Perloff, "Charles Olson," p. 294.

20. See Marcia Lieberman and Philip Lieberman, "Olson's Projective Verse and the Use of Breath Control as a Structural Element," *Language and Style* 5 (Fall 1972); 287–98.

21. I. A. Richards, *Mencius on the Mind* (London: Routledge & Kegan Paul, 1964), p. 8.

22. Fielding Dawson says, "Charley was possessed by his voice . . . if you want to understand Charley's poems, he's talking" (quoted by Sherman Paul, *Olson's Push* [Baton Rouge, La.: Louisiana State University Press, 1978], p. 118).

23. See Jane Harrison, *Ancient Art and Ritual* (London: Thornton Butterworth, Ltd., 1913), p. 35, and Olson's commentary (*SVH*, 21–23).

24. Harrison, *Ancient Art and Ritual*, p. 35.

25. (Princeton, N.J.: Princeton University Press, 1949). This is one of the most heavily annotated texts in Olson's library.

26. Olson read this quotation in Weyl, *Philosophy of Mathematics and Natural Science*, p. 105.

27. Ibid., p. 43.

28. Ibid., p. 72.

29. H. Graham Flegg, *From Geometry to Topology* (London: English Universities Press, 1974), p. 17.

3

"The Kingfishers": Charles Olson's "Marvelous Maneuver"

> O, they were hot for the world they
> lived in, these Maya, hot to get it down
> the way it was—the way it is, my fellow
> citizens.
> —*Human Universe and Other Essays*

Charles Olson wrote "The Kingfishers" in 1949 when his "stance toward reality" was quickening. Soon he would codify that stance and the principles of its expression in two position papers, "The Human Universe" and "Projective Verse," but in "The Kingfishers" we have perhaps the most dense rendering of the Olson posture. Later, in *The Maximus Poems*, the density would attenuate and the method would lose some of its aggressive presence, but in this earlier, briefer effort we have the advantage of a concentrate. The poem is Olson distilled, form obediently extending from content, a reliable index to the dogmatic complexity of its author. As Olson himself once put it, "If you don't know Kingfishers you don't have a starter" (*LO*, 63).

Seeking to "know" "Kingfishers," as opposed to feeling its intensity as kinetic experience, may seem suspiciously untoward as an approach to an Olson poem, even as a "starter," since it implies a conceptual attitude toward an enterprise dedicated to the resistance of all "irritable reaching after fact and reason." On the other hand, knowing something of the principles and materials that inform the poem may help us see how valuable it is as a

gauge not only of the mind and energy of the Olson who
wrote it but of the Olson to come later. "The Kingfishers"
is, to use an expression Olson borrowed from Franz Kline,
a "marvellous maneuver," the result of "a writer's ability to
get will ass-backwards—in that wonderful sense that one
does what one knows before one knows what one does."[1]
In "The Kingfishers" Olson did what he only later fully
knew,[2] and the poem's consistency with intellectual positions he was to codify in the future is testimony to the
trustworthiness of what Olson has called "blind obedience"
to "personage," that is, the belief that "each of us is more
than a physiology or a will ... [that] we are also an obedience. And what we obey—have to obey—is something we
are in the hands of, not in our own hands alone. I refer to
the life in us."[3]

As an act of obedience to the life in Olson, "The
Kingfishers" poses interpretive problems for those unac-
quainted with the direction in which its author's energies
move. For example, it has been oddly fashionable for critics to admire "The Kingfishers" as a literary polemic.
"Olson, in 'The Kingfishers,'" writes one, "is launching ...
an all-out attack on Eliot; ostensibly addressing himself to
the problem of a shifting political reality (the dichotomy
between East and West) he uses the political situation as an
example of the inadequacy of Christianity."[4] Unfortu-
nately, this argument begins to cohere only if passages
quoted directly from Plutarch are attributed instead to
Eliot and if Olson's widely expressed cultural opinions are
totally ignored. Presumably the quotation from Mao trig-
gers the notion that "The Kingfishers" deals with shifting
political realities, but in fact the poem is political only in
the broadest sense of what Olson intends by the term *polis*.
Since Christianity is not remotely alluded to in the poem, it
can only be assumed it was smuggled in on Eliot's coattails.

Another reader, after singling out the "inhibiting example of M. L. Rosenthal [as] the one critic who has dealt with
Olson's poetry at any length and who seems not to have
understood it, missing altogether the strong vein of
parody in 'The Kingfishers.'" seems equally insistent to

reduce the poem to a contretemps with Eliot. The poem, he declares, is "directed against the mystique of Eliot and full of echoes from the *Four Quartets*. In the very first line of this poem Olson limits Eliot's concept of the changeless moment: 'What does not change / is the will to change.'" He goes on to say, "Olson uses Eliot's Heraclitan allusions for his own purposes. . . . [and] also uses Eliot's language of dessication: 'And, considering the dryness of the place / the long absence of an adequate race / . . .we must rise, act.'"[5]

Why it must be Eliot's "changeless moment" that Olson limits (if that was Olson's intention at all) is difficult to discern. The assumption seems to be that Eliot holds exclusive franchise on all "changeless moments,"Heraclitean fragments, dryness, and organic process philosophy. The passage cited as Eliot's Heraclitean allusion is, in fact, directly quoted from Plutarch,[6] and the so-called language of dessication is actually owing to a geographical description of Chichén Itzá by the noted anthropologist Sir Eric Thompson.[7] Finally, "we must arise, act" is attributed in the poem itself to Mao: "nous devons / nous lever / et agir!"

Rosenthal's reading shows a considerably greater acquaintance with Olson's concerns and his methodology. Isolating the three major motifs that run through "The Kingfishers" (the ancient symbol "E"; the quotation from Mao; and the overall symbol of the kingfisher), he acknowledges the "crucial issue" of the poem as the "betrayal of humanly meaningful modes of life that were discovered before the emergence of the modern state."[8] Aside from the word "betrayal," which perhaps intrudes an overly moral ingredient into Olson's organic view of cultural history, Rosenthal's précis is not inconsistent with the cultural position that Olson's works and marginalia yield. That position, an amalgam of his broad reading, can be suggested through a few pertinent quotations. The first comes from Olson's heavily annotated copy of Brooks Adams's *The Law of Civilization and Decay*, which is also notable for its high recommendation in *A Bibliography on America for*

Ed Dorn.[9] Adams asserts that "when a highly centralized society disintegrates, under the pressure of economic competition, it is because the energy of the race has been exhausted. Consequently, the survivors of such a community lack the power necessary for renewed concentration, and most probably remain inert until supplied with fresh energetic material."[10]

Olson tends to interpret Adams's "racial energy" in Jungian terms that correspond to his own principle of "blind obedience" to the "life in us." In his copy of *The Integration of the Personality* is his heavily underlined passage: "The anima is a 'factor' in the proper sense of the word. Man cannot make it; on the contrary, it is always the *a priori* element in moods, reactions, impulses and whatever else is spontaneous in psychic life. It is something that lives on its own account, that makes us live; it is a life behind unconsciousness."[11] In Jung, as in Adams, Olson finds a principle of energy, racial or psychic, which is both within and beyond man—an energy precisely equivalent to what he labels the "life in us"—available for obedience.

A third quotation, from Olson's unpublished essay, "The Mystery" (*CTU*), suggests how "lost" energy can be recovered from the primordial matrix through creative act. Melville, Olson declares, "recovered processes of the imagination and tapped reservoirs of image and feeling which are essentially primordial and thus, on the technical side, precede print. It is his revolution in the sense of recovery rather than advance that leads me to call him mythographer rather than writer."

Adams's "racial energy," Jung's "archetypal anima," and Melville's creative "recovery" of primordial energy through image and feeling supply an outline of the cultural point of view animating "The Kingfishers." It is a view that recommends the repossession of a lost, pre-Socratic "stance toward reality" (elsewhere called by Olson the "will to cohere" [*HU*, 21]) that unburdens man of the abstractions of Greek rationalism by placing him in a posture obedient to the rhythms of the "life in us." The particular intensity of "The Kingfishers" generates from Olson's conviction that the "recovery" is now at hand as a real cultural possibility for America:

> Now I spend most of my time studying the Sumerians and Mayans. . . . The will to cohere in both these people is what I can see in us, in now. I do not mean collectivism, though I am not at all so uncomfortable in the face of it, and of quantity, as those of my contemporaries seem to be who are stuck with the old soul, and quality, and who back up, for sanctions, to those walls which have been a comfort for man in the East and the West since 1500 B.C. (The American Indian lies outside that comfortable box just as much, I'd argue, as the Americans now do, despite Western appearance. I meant it, in *Ishmael*, that we are the last first people.) [*AP*, 40]

Like his literary guru, Melville, Olson feels himself in a revolution of "recovery rather than advance" and senses the inadequacy of the term *writer* to comprehend his quest. "I find it awkward to call myself a poet or a writer," he confesses. "If there are no walls there are no names. . . . I am an archeologist of morning. And the writing and acts which I find bear on the present job are . . . from Homer back, not forward" (*AP*, 40). "The Kingfishers" is a product of that anthropological commitment to the recovery of a pre-Greek orientation, and it is no dishonor to consider the poem less an utterance of Olson the poet than the potent statement of Olson the archeologist.

Not only does the poem open with the ruins of ancient Angkor Vat, take us through a series of quick cuts of Mayan ritual, and investigate relics and burial vaults, but it closes with a paraphrase of Rimbaud's "Fêtes de la Faim," which turns out ultimately to be a prophetic declaration of Olson's intention to launch an archeological expedition of his own:

> if I have any taste
> it is only because I have interested myself
> in what was slain in the sun

I pose you your question:

shall you uncover honey / where maggots
        are?

I hunt among stones

                       (*D*, 11)

The "honey" attracting Olson's "taste" lies in the residue of
the ancient Mayan empire, particularly among the stone
hieroglyphs that originally caught his interest as the expression of a civilization "anterior"[12] to the Greek in which
Western civilization is rooted. The Maya were literally
"slain in the sun," and Olson is convinced that the energy
which nourished their great civilization can be repossessed
through the latent power of the glyphs and also through
the love, sensed in the very flesh, of the present-day Maya.

"The Human Universe" explicitly relates Olson's taste
for Mayan civilization to his position:

> I have found that the hieroglyphs of the Maya disclose a
> placement of themselves towards nature of enormous
> contradiction to ourselves. . . . Man has made himself an
> ugliness and a bore. It was better to be a bird, as these
> Maya seem to have been, they kept moving their heads
> so nervously to stay alive, to keep alerted to what they
> were surrounded by. . . . O, they were hot for the world
> they lived in, these Maya, hot to get it down the way it
> was—the way it is, my fellow citizens. (*HU*, 15)

The way it "was" and "is" (could be) is the orientation from
which Western man has been alienated since the advent of
Greek humanism (logic, classification, and idealism), a
humanism (dubbed "discourse" by Olson) that has estranged man "from that which was most familiar" (*M*, 52).
In Yucatan, as Creeley points out, "the alternative to a
generalizing humanism was locked, quite literally, in the
people" (*ML*, 5–6), and it is to these people that Olson optimistically precommits himself in "The Kingfishers":

> But I have my kin, if for no other reason than
> (as he said, next of kin) I commit myself, and,
> given my freedom, I'd be a cad
> if I didn't. Which is most true.
>
> (D, 11)

The poem opens with an ontological dogma: "What does not change / is the will to change." The line finds a specific context later (Part I, section 4) in material Olson quotes from Plutarch; its appearance here is as a controlling text. While assuming the Heraclitean axiom exploited by Plutarch that all is flux, its emphasis rhythmically and conceptually falls on the word "will," the "*will* to change" (italics mine). Olson's explicit definition of will, "the innate voluntarism to live . . . the infinitive of being," proposed in *The Special View of History* (p. 44), would rule out any notion that human existence is helplessly at the mercy of change. To the contrary, Olson insists that "man does influence external reality" (*HU*, 11), but he consistently points out that there are at least "two sorts of will" that he identifies at the cultural level as the "will to cohere" and the will to "disperse" (*HU*, 21), and at the individual level as the " will of power" and the "will of achievement" (*SVH*, 45).

Power and *achievement* are terms borrowed from Keats, and the will of power, as Olson explains it, "tries to make it by asserting the self as character. The second makes it by non-asserting the self as self. In other words the riddle is that the true self is not the asserting function but an obeying one, that the actionable is *larger* than the individual and so can be obeyed to" (*SVH*, 45). Olson thus assimilates Keats's terms into his principle of "blind obedience" to "personage" and, although the "life in us" is now called the "actionable," the principle that one ought to assume an obedient rather than an assertive role toward natural process remains the same. Olson links his position even closer to Keats's by incorporating into it the principle of negative capability:

> To stay in mysteries, uncertainties, doubts . . . is Keats'
> way of talking about staying in process in order to

realize the ontogenetic in the face of the phylogenetic, not to slip into the error of trying to fix things by an ir- ritable reaching after fact and reason . . . which is man's tease to know by stopping. . . . And he can't; if he stops it he gets a half, which will turn out to be only his proper self or his ego or Character, an imposition, POWER. (*SVH*, 42)

The changeless "will to change," then, might be seen as a recommended position in the face of universal flux, a po- sition that is comfortable with mystery, content in process and devoid of "irritable reaching after fact and reason." It is a position in which the will is obedient to the larger force of process, neither assertive nor egocentric, and yet one that "achieves" because it taps the energy of the "action- able." It is the kind of flexible position that Brooks Adams sees in successful civilizations:

All administrative systems tend toward induration; more especially political systems, because they are most cumbersome. Conversely, nature is in eternal move- ment. Therefore the disparity between any given gov- ernment and its environment is apt to be proportionate to the time which has elapsed since the last period of ac- tive change. When a population is flexible, adjustment is peaceful . . .; when a population is rigid, a catastrophe occurs.[13]

The announcement that opens "The Kingfishers" is thus both an explanation and a challenge. It accounts for the rise and fall of civilizations, but it also advises that the cultural consequences are in man's control: he can choose to assert or obey, disperse or cohere, impose or achieve. The poem generates energy from the conflict between these options.

The next narrative portion of section 1 strives to present a context from which Fernand's question, "The pool the kingfishers' feathers were wealth why / did the export stop?" can pick up enough metaphysical significance to support the philosophical theme of the poem, for it seems plausible that the query which closes "The Kingfishers" ("shall you uncover honey / where maggots are?") is intended as a kind of answering counter-question to the one Fernand poses here. At any rate, the remembered events of a party are all related to archeology. Fernand, the enigmatic center of interest, is presumably an archeologist of sorts himself. Although he is profoundly disturbed by the eroded value of kingfisher feathers, it is not clear whether his concern is aesthetic, economic, or even pedantic. On the one hand, as he mutters over and over to a circle of "smirking" listeners, "the kingfishers' feathers were wealth why / did the export stop?" he appears baffled by what seems to him an economic anomaly, but earlier, when he asserts, "'The pool is slime!'" and "'The kingfishers! / who cares / for their feathers / now?'" he seems deeply moved by an immense and deplorable collapse of aesthetic value. The narrator's surmise that Fernand left the party to lose "himself / in some crack in the ruins" obscures things more by hinting at an archeological pedantry in his makeup. The central enigma of Fernand, however, originates from the undercutting of his apparent aesthetic concern by an oddly materialistic diction.

If the conceptual impact of Fernand is diffuse, his kinetic presence is nevertheless potent. We sense the genuineness of his concern, we feel the depth of his disillusionment with the present, and we grasp the urgency of his appeal. We could explain away the conceptual untidiness of the aesthetic-economic tension as a concession to realism—that is the way people talk at parties—but a more plausible reconciliation of these aesthetic and economic concerns is available in the Brooks Adams excerpt quoted earlier: "When a highly centralized society disintegrates, under the pressure of economic competition, it is because the energy of the race has been exhausted." Within the context of Adams's cultural theory the cessation of the export of feathers is not merely an economic phenomenon but announces the exhaustion of racial energy. "Why did the export stop?" thus becomes a cultural puzzle of considerable metaphysical weight and suggests that archeology holds promise of a solution.

The riddle of why the kingfisher feathers have lost their value calls to the narrator's mind a parallel cultural conundrum, the "E on the stone." The E is the mysterious sign in the entry of the temple at Delphi, but Olson's allusion also includes Plutarch's essay, "The E at Delphi," which attempts to probe its meaning. Just as the kingfisher feathers were the subject of cultural speculation for Fernand and his smirking listeners, so the E serves as puzzle for Plutarch's symposiasts who methodically apply the logical procedures of "discourse" in order to attain "an explanation of the unexplainable."[14] Their inability to penetrate the mystery satisfactorily with the epistemological machinery at hand prompts the moderator, Ammonius, to supply an alternative ontological context: that "nothing is either stable or existing, but all things are being born or perishing, according to their distribution with respect to time."[15] Within a context of flux instead of analytical repose, Ammonius is able to conclude that the E means "Thou art," a salute and acknowledgment of God's eternal Being within a universe of finite Becoming. Thus Ammonius appears to champion a Heraclitean ontology in the face of the assumptions of "discourse" that "estrange" man "from that with which he is most familiar." Olson considers Ammonius's presentation of the ontology of process so crucial that he fashions from it the substance of section 4 of "The Kingfishers."

In this section, however, the moral seems to be that such mysteries as feathers and Es are impervious to a discursive, analytical stance because their real significance is rooted in a primordial matrix. This is why in section 3 Olson says, "the E / cut so rudely on the oldest stone / sounded otherwise, / was differently heard." The epistemological assumptions of one culture may be useless in sounding the assumptions of another, particularly when one, Greek "discourse," "intermit[s] our participation in our experience, and so prevent[s] discovery" (*HU*, 4).

The thought of the E is accompanied by the recollection of an excerpt from Mao's 1948 Report to his Party, which is straightaway placed in serial opposition with the legend accounting for the kingfisher's red breast. Mao and the legend thus serve as poles for a series of corollary oppositions: East versus West, the rising versus the setting sun, and fact versus myth. The E and the legend together contrast with Mao and his activist speech in terms of time, geography, expression, and counsel. On the one hand, we have ancient Western myth pleading a return to a pre-Socratic cultural stance; on the other hand, a contemporary Eastern realism calling for assertive, popular power. Not only does one sense in this contrast the will to cohere versus the will to disperse and the man of achievement versus the man of power, but the two options are precisely those Olson saw facing Mexico. "'I have no doubt, say, that the American will more and more repossess himself of the Indian past,'" he wrote to Creely from Campeche.

> "If you and I see the old deal as dead (including Confucius, say), at the same time that we admit the new is of the making of our own lives & references, yet, there is bound to be a tremendous pick-up from history other than that which has been usable as reference, the moment either that history is restored (Sumer, or, more done, Chichen or Uaxactun) or rising people (these Indians, as campesinos ripe for Communist play—as ripe as were the Chinese, date 1921, June 30)."(ML, 6)

One recalls Olson's praise of Herman Melville's revolution as one of "recovery rather than advance." Here, the options appear the same: the "recovery" or "pick-up from history" set up against the activist advance urged by Mao.

In Part II these options are considered again:

> The light is in the east. Yes. And we must rise, act.
> Yet in the west, despite the apparent darkness. . . .

What follows is an elliptical invitation to examine with candor the cultural energy residually evident not only in the Mayan ruins themselves but in the descendents of those Mayan kings. Although Olson concedes the pragmatic inevitability of Mao's activism, he nevertheless cleaves to his own "differently heard" assessment, anticipating, as he does so, the poem's final resolution: "I hunt among stones."

The most interesting contrast is between fact and myth. Olson's well-known reverence for myth and legend stems from the act that these expressions, unlike the abstractions of "discourse," contain in them a collective sense of human relevance. A thing's "self-existence" is its most important fact, Olson believed, and "this is what we are confronted by, not the thing's 'class,' any hierarchy, of quality or quantity, but the thing itself, and its *relevance* to ourselves who are the experience of it" (*HU*, 6). Legend provides "self-existence" and "human relevance" in particularly coherent form, and this is why, after a detailed, analytical description of the kingfisher borrowed from the *Encyclopaedia Britannica*, Olson intrudes,

> But not these things were the factors. Not the birds.
> The legends are
> legends. . . .

The pause forced by the line-break after "are" is hermeneutically potent, for it creates a parasyntactical logic that momentarily asserts that the legends, not the birds, are the factors. This is Olson's primary point: the bird's "self-existence" and its "relevance to ourselves," not ornithological data, are what count. In other words, the " reality" of the birds must be mythically presented.

On the other hand, the syntactically dictated reading, "The legends are / legends," is significant in another way in that from the point of view of "discourse," legends are simply that—legends: quaint, amusing, but pragmatically useless fictions. Accordingly, the rest of the passage lists a series of tedious negations of legend all justified, apparently, on the basis of analytical fact. The moral seems clear enough: "discourse" reduces reality to a single, coherent line of sight; legend takes it in whole.

Discursively legendless, the life cycle of kingfishers is bleak:

> On these rejectamenta
> (as they accumulate they form a cup-shaped
>   structure) the
>   young are born.
> And, as they are fed and grow, this nest of excrement
>   and
>   decayed fish becomes
>   a dripping fetid mass

The grim "realities" uncovered by "discourse" ("rejec-tamenta," "excrement," "fetid mass") vividly contrast with the "realities" of myth ("he got the color of his breast / from the heat of the setting sun!"), and it is tempting to speculate that Olson saw in this depressingly reductionist quotation a paradigm for the Western cultural predicament. The nest, for instance, serves as an emblem for time. In a passage underlined by Olson in "The E at Delphi," Plutarch strikingly defines time as "leaking and not holding water, as it were, a vessel full of decay and growth."[16] Olson's intimacy with this passage suggests that the association between the nest and Plutarch's "vessel" is more than coincidental. If the nest figures a human or cultural life span, one established on the accumulated "rejec-tamenta" of what has passed, the fact that the result is a "dripping, fetid mass" or a "pool of slime" suggests a cultural stagnation brought about most probably by the effort of "discourse" to stop the flux. The word "accumulation" has particular significance here, for Olson often uses it to describe, pejoratively, the basic assumptions of "discourse": that knowledge and experience accumulate rather than change. Section 4, for example, opens with the counsel: "not accumulation but change."

Whatever the cause, the cultural "pejorocracy" of the West is diagnosed as "a pool of slime" and a "dripping fetid mass." A prescription is clearly called for and, for the moment, Mao is permitted to supply it:

>   nous devons
>   nous lever
>   et agir!

Maintaining a vital stance toward reality is indeed summed up in the single word "attention," which Olson emphasizes in the controlling text of section 3:

> When the attentions change / the jungle
> leaps in
>   even the stones are split
>   they rive

Although his reference is to *The Maximus Poems*, J. B. Philip speaks of Olson's particular use of the words "attention" and "care," how "'attention' to context in which they live . . . [and] a particular 'care' for the quality and management of their community . . . [provide for the 'polis' of Gloucester the] experience of community as one of 'touch all round.'"[17] Olson speaks of the "continuing struggle to remain civilized" in "The Gate and the Center," and warns of what happens when the "best of men . . . lose touch with the primordial & phallic energies & methodologies which . . . make it possible for man . . . to take up, straight, . . . nature's force" (*HU*, 23). "Attention" and "care" to one's stance toward "nature's force," "personage," the "life in us," "process," or any of the other labels Olson gives to "what we obey" is a daily cultural obligation, for when the attention slackens, so does the will to cohere.

The allusion to the Spanish "conqueror" who "so resembles ourselves" shows that slackening attention not only invites natural erosion of civilization but also military invasion and economic exploitation. Olson was undoubtedly impressed by Brooks Adams's remark (noted in his copy of *The New Empire*) that "the soldier is a natural force, like the flood or the whirlwind,"[18] but perhaps even more telling on the Mayan civilization was the deadly infusion of "discourse" brought about by the conquistadors. The primordial sign *E* is again introduced to suggest the cultural sea change that occurred with the conquest. Just as the original meaning of the E sounded "otherwise" and was "differently heard" by Plutarch's symposiasts, so does Mayan treasure undergo a shift in significance. To illustrate the point, Olson included what is apparently a catalogue of

Mayan icons richly worked in gold. In the catalogue the word *gold* is emphasized through placement and repetition (the word itself is used five times). In the original Mayan culture, gold was exclusively superintended by the priests and used for ceremonial purposes. When the conquistador invaded, the priests, "their dishevelled hair matted with blood,"[19] rushed in among the people to try to get them to save their gods (the focus of their cultural integrity). As the "attention" toward gold changed from a substance valued for its ceremonial significance to a commodity whose value was assigned from without, a grim transition took place from an attentively poised and coherent culture to one which was dispersed by acquisitiveness and "discourse":

> And all now is war
> where so lately there was peace,
> and the sweet brotherhood, the use
> of tilled fields.[20]

The concluding section of Part I is appropriately philosophic—even didactic. Principles that up to this point have been presented for intuitive and visceral absorption are now more conceptually defined through the borrowings from Plutarch. In addition to the Plutarch material, however, Olson adds some significant embellishments from Norbert Wiener's *Cybernetics; or, Control and Communication in the Animal and the Machine*,[21] the subtitle of which is directly quoted in the poem. From Wiener's book Olson takes the term *feedback* and declares it a law. In *Cybernetics and Society* Wiener defined feedback as "a method of controlling a system by reinserting into it the results of its past performance,"[22] but Olson's interest in the term is in its application to epistemology: as the technique man employs for obedience to "nature's force." In a universe of process, of incessant change, man must assume a posture that will tap rather than obstruct the inherent energy of that change. The position is spelled out in "The Human Universe":

There is only one thing you can do about kinetic, re-
enact it.... And if man is once more to possess intent in
his life, and to take up the responsibility implicit in his
life, he has to comprehend his own process as intact,
from outside, by way of his skin, in, and by his own powers of conversion, out again.... Man's action ... (when
it is good) is the equal of all intake plus all transpos-
ing.... It is the equal of its cause only when it proceeds
unbroken from the threshold of a man through him
and back out again, without loss of quality, to the external world from which it came. (*HU*, 10–11)

The law of feedback is most demonstrable in man's creative acts. There his obligation is to create or "feed back"
objects that are "equal to the real itself," and that is why
Olson insists that "art is the only twin life has—its only
valid metaphysic (*HU*, 10). If art is the means for reenact-
ing or "twinning" life, then the "factors," which in section 2
were unclear, can now be appreciated as the factors in
capturing reality in process; "We can be precise" in talking
about them:

> The factors are
> in the animal and/or the machine the factors are
> communication and/or control, both involve
> the message. And what is the message? The message
> is
> a discrete or continuous sequence of measurable
> events
> distributed in time

Communication, Olson seems to be implying through this
mosaic of quotations from Wiener,[23] is our feedback to
external reality. It is also plausible that Wiener's words attracted Olson's attention because of their applicability to
his pet observation, enunciated in "Projective Verse," that
"it is the advantage of the typewriter that, due to its rigidity
and its space precisions, it can, for a poet, indicate exactly
the breath, the pauses, the suspensions even of syllables,

the juxtapositions even of parts of phrases, which he intends" (*HU*, 57). The typewriter synthesizes animal and machine into a comprehensive message. The message? It is literally as Wiener asserts it: "The message is a discrete or continuous sequence of measurable events distributed in time"—the definition of reality dictated by process philosophy. Plutarch articulates it with more fullness:

> And if Nature, when it is measured, is subject to the same processes as is the agent that measures it, then there is nothing in Nature that has permanence or even existence, but all things are in the process of creation or destruction according to their relative distribution with respect to time.[24]

In a universe of ever-shifting relationships, where one moment's description of a thing is nullified by the new constellation of the next moment, reality is indeed hopelessly elusive; "the too strong grasping of it" obviously "loses it," and the only conceivable way of dealing with it is through corresponding motion. For this reason Olson's work may to some seem circular and repetitive, a charge Olson readily admits.[25] His art, as it "twins" reality, must keep moving abreast with what is going on, forging ahead in a circular envelopment of the subject, never emending, never changing, but, true to the process of his activity, keeping up with the moment and "feeding back" what comes at him fresh at the threshold of the skin. This is the law of feedback, the law of Olson's art.

Part II begins with the familiar theme of birth and death again, although here it is rendered through specifically factual details of Mayan burial and baptism ceremonies. Once more, a parallelism with the description of the kingfisher's nest is irresistible; the underground tomb recalling the "end of a tunnel bored . . . in a bank" where the kingfisher nests, and the sepulchral bones reminding us of the "rejectamenta," the "bones thrown up in pellets by the birds." Again, the opposition of East and West is presented, but this time with a stronger recommendation that the Mayan past holds valuable secrets for the present. Despite the "apparent darkness" that Olson sees shrouding modern Western civilization, the "whiteness / which covers all," if we take the trouble to "look," there is eventually to be discovered a "light" and a "flower." The "apparent darkness" refers primarily to the violent sacrificial rituals of the Maya, but it also alludes to the darkening effects of "discourse" upon the West. Underneath this apparent dark whiteness is to be found salvageable value—that of an alternative culture to the Greek. "Whiteness" literally describes the Mayan edifices. Sir Eric Thompson, for example, notes that "a Mayan city shone in the sun with a dazzling whiteness, since every wall, staircase, and floor was covered with stucco, usually creamy white, but sometimes red."[26] Olson probably also had in mind Fenollosa's damning phrase, "the dead white plaster of the copula,"[27] which would provide the link between whiteness and Greek "discourse."

The narrator's plea, at any rate, is that we look forbearingly into the whiteness of the face of the Mayan ruins with candor, and that in our examination we allow tolerance for "the dryness of the place" (no Eliotic desiccation here, but literally the well-documented dryness of Campeche and Yucatan that made the cultural success of the Maya so spectacular, particularly their achievement in domesticating maize).[28] Consideration is also asked for "the long absence of an adequate race." Again, the literal supplies clarification. In "The Human Universe" Olson concedes that the descendants of the Maya "have gone down before the poundings of our way" and are "poor failures of the modern world, incompetent to arrange that in the month of June, when the rains have not yet come far enough forward to fill the wells, they have water to wash in or to drink" (*HU*, 6).

We should not excuse the conquistadors' destruction of Mayan idols on grounds that the idols were "black" from sacrificial "human gore."[29] To the contrary, we are requested to "hear, where the dry blood talks / where the old appetite walks." Rather than blinding our understanding

with moral judgments, we should "look" with candor beneath the dark violence of Mayan ritual and "hear" the
primordial reality of "the old appetite." The appetite can
still be found; it "hides" in the "eye" of the present-day
Maya and "runs in [their] flesh / chalk [the chalk of the
glyphs]."

The curious line "whence it arose" bafflingly seems to
suggest that the "old appetite" hidden in ancient Mayan
culture somehow "arose," presumably to some other-
worldly reality. "The Kingfishers" itself provides little assistance toward clarifying this enigmatic phrase, but in
"The Praises," which Olson considered a companion piece
to "The Kingfishers," the phrase appears again in con-
junction with the myth of how the Sun, originally mortal, is
enticed into the heavens by the Moon. Olson's admitted
euhemerism causes him to conjecture in "The Gate and
the Center," "How many generations does it take to turn a
hero into a God?" (*HU*, 17) and it would appear as though
he tentatively intended to connect anthropological history
and religious mythology. A letter to Creeley indicates that
he abandoned the development of the assertion in "The
Kingfishers," even though this residue of the notion remains in the poem:

> It is (you see, I am still harping on this problem of mine,
> reference: constellations, Venus included (which, here,
> I will show can be called KuKulCan—abandoned such,
> as part of THE K'S and THE PRAISES, discovering this
> man's death [KuKulCan's], April 5, 1208 AD, who "rose"
> with Venus, 8 days later. (*ML*, 17)

Kukulcan was the real or legendary leader of the Itzá who
occupied Chichén Itzá from A.D. 968 to 987. The feath-
ered serpent god, Quetzalcoatl, became identified with
Kukulcan, which presumably excited Olson's euhemeristic
belief that Kukulcan did indeed become elevated to a god.

Olson's apparent admiration for the "old appetite"and
his disdain for those who would excuse the conquistadors'
destruction of the Mayan culture on the grounds that it

was violent, bloody, and harsh reinforces the fact that what
he culturally values is not ethically but aesthetically ad-
mired. "Art is the only morality" (*LO*, 106), he once wrote
to Cid Corman, and this conviction helps us to appreciate
the kinetic tension with which aesthetic and moral virtues
are counterpoised in the final two stanzas of Part II:

> with what violence benevolence is bought
> what cost in gesture justice brings
> what wrongs domestic rights involve
> what stalks
> this silence
>
> what pudor pejorocracy affronts
> how awe, night-rest and neighborhood can rot
> what breeds where dirtiness is law
> what crawls
> below

Primordial power is measured against social "enlighten-
ment" in a kind of Heraclitean acknowledgment that "it is
by disease that health is pleasant; by evil that good is pleasant; by hunger, satiety; by weariness, rest."[30] The oppositions imply an inevitable trade-off: beauty at the expense
of justice and vice versa. "Dirtiness" becomes law, presumably, when the oppositions are not seen as natural conditions of the flux but as pressing either/or options. The law,
as Olson instructs, is "feed-back"—"staying in process,"
remaining "obedient" to the "actionable," and avoiding all
"irritable grasping after fact and reason." "If man is active," Olson says, "it is exactly here where experience
comes in that it is delivered back, and if he stays fresh at
the coming in he will be fresh at the going out." The fail-
ure of the attention to safeguard that freshness results in
"slime," the "fetid nest," "maggots," and all the other ready
images of pejorocracy.

It is no wonder, then, that the final part of "The
Kingfishers" sarcastically disavows its culture's classical
roots, both temperamentally and syntactically,[31] on the
basis that it "can take no risk that matters, / the risk of

beauty least of all." For Olson, at least, the ending is a forcefully personal one. Whatever others choose to do, he has found his "kin," the Maya, to whom he freely commits himself. With Rimbaud, he fixes his taste to phenomena, "la terre et les pierres," and dedicates himself to the search for honey among the stones.

Like its subject matter, the form of "The Kingfishers" is a function of process and bears all the idiosyncrasies that accrue from that fact. What Robert von Hallberg says of the "serial, open form" of *The Maximus Poems* is equally true of "The Kingfishers":

> It encourages repetition, parenthesis, and apposition. Because nothing can be stated exactly and finally, one must try to say something once, be dissatisfied at the incompleteness of expression, try to say again more completely, be again dissatisfied, and so on, in theory at least, *ad infinitum*.[32]

As if cleaving to its own injunction, "not accumulation but change," "The Kingfishers" does say the same things over and over in its sections, but each time from a different vantage point of space, time, and perception. We have seen recurring figures metamorphize in response to the changed conditions in which they are reconceived: a "pool" changes to a "nest"; from "nest" it changes to a vessel for time; finally it reappears as a burial vault. Similarly, "slime" transposes into "rejectamenta," then to "mongolian louse," then to "maggots," and finally to a generalized "what crawls below." No matter what the figure, the poet's obedience to the energies flowing through him in the feedback process assures its coherence—even its reality. Restricting his responsibility to the act of "attention," to "staying fresh at the coming in and the going out," he remains confident all the while that if he does only this the poem will take care of itself. This is the logic, of course, of "composition by field" and the rationale behind Olson's admission that when he writes a poem, "I don't know what I am up to! And must stay in that state in order to accomplish what I have to do."[33]

"The Kingfishers" was written before "The Gate and the Center," "The Human Universe," *The Special View of History*, and Olson's other statements of cultural position. It preceded Olson's knowledge of the metaphysics of Whitehead that so significantly structures his later work and thought. Nevertheless, the poem's intuitive obedience to the stance toward reality codified for Olson six years later by Whitehead is such that it is a passage from *Process and Reality* (unknown to Olson at the time "The Kingfishers" was written)[34] that best summarizes its theme:

> The social history of mankind exhibits great organizations in their alternating functions of conditions for progress, and of contrivances for stunting humanity. The history of the Mediterranean lands, and of western Europe, is the history of the blessing and the curse, of political organizations, of religious organizations, of schemes of thought, of social agencies for large purposes. The moment of dominance, prayed for, worked for, sacrificed for, by generations of the noblest spirits, marks the turning point where the blessing passes into the curse. Some new principle of refreshment is required. The art of progress is to preserve order amid change, and to preserve change amid order. Life refuses to be embalmed alive. The more prolonged the halt in some unrelieved system of order, the greater the crash of the dead society.[35]

Marginalia in Olson's copy of "The E at Delphi," scribbled in ten years after he wrote "The Kingfishers," reveals the confirming impact of his subsequent knowledge of Whitehead. Ammonius's allusion to the famous Heraclitean remark, "It is not possible to step into the same river twice," receives Olson's arrowed note, "Add Whitehead." Similarly, to Ammonius's assertion (underlined by Olson) that "Reason distributes too much, dissolves and destroys," we find Olson's margin notation: "Right: connect via wh's 10 seconds of the 'actual' occasion."[36]

The impression one gets is that of a man reviewing earlier intimations with the advantage of a validating metaphysics. Olson was, after all, a teacher with a natural pedagogic urge to structure truths as much as he dared for classroom consumption. Copies of his lectures—*The Special View of History*, for example—demonstrate his penchant for schematics and classifications in spite of his diatribe against "discourse." The point is that Olson's natural progress seems to be from felt intuition to codified exposition without appreciable loss of the content's integrity: from "The Kingfishers," say, to *The Special View of History*. All this is by way of reaffirming that Olson, as poet-archeologist-teacher-metaphysician, was the master of the "marvelous maneuver"; he did what he knew before he knew what he did.

NOTES

1. Ann Charters, *Olson/Melville: A Study in Affinity* (Berkeley, Calif.: Oyez, 1968), p. 86.
2. This statement is based upon Olson's marginalia inscribed, ten years after the writing of "The Kingfishers," in several volumes in his private library but most particularly in his copy of *Plutarch's Morals*, from which he directly quoted much of the material in Part I, section 4 of the poem. The issue is discussed more fully later.
3. Unpublished lecture entitled "To Make It Clear," contained in the "Institute I" folder in the Charles Olson Archives, University of Connecticut (hereafter referred to by the Library of Congress abbreviation CtU). Excerpts from Charles Olson's works and marginalia are copyrighted by the Estate of Charles Olson and are used here by permission.
4. Maxine Combs, "Charles Olson's 'The Kingfishers': A Consideration of Meaning and Method," *Far Point* 4 (Spring/Summer 1970), p. 68.
5. William Aiken, "Charles Olson: A Preface," *Massachusetts Review* 12 (Winter 1971): 58–59.
6. See *Plutarch's Moralia*, trans. C. W. King (London: George Bell and Sons, 1908), p. 192.
7. See Sir Eric Thompson, *Civilization of the Mayas*, 4th ed., No. 25 (Chicago: Field Museum of Natural History, University of Chicago Department of Anthropology, 1942), p. 17 et passim; also *Maya Hieroglyphic Writing: Introduction*, publication 589 (Washington, D.C.: Carnegie Institution of Washington, 1950): "The Northern Area, the third division, comprises Yucatan and most of Campeche and Quintana Roo.... The annual rainfall averages a scant 45 cm.... This greater aridity is reflected in the vegetation which becomes more scrublike as one goes northward.... Much of the land

would be quite waterless were it not that in places the surface crust of limestone has caved in giving access to deposits of water beneath [cenotes]" (p. 4). This volume is part of Olson's private library.

8. M. L. Rosenthal, *The New Poets: American and British Poetry Since World War II* (New York: Oxford University Press, 1967), pp. 160–61. A more recent essay on "The Kingfishers" and an invaluable guide to many of its allusions is Guy Davenport's "Scholia and Conjectures for Olson's 'The Kingfishers,'" *Boundary 2* 2 (Fall 1973/Winter 1974): 250–62. Sherman Paul provides a relatively full exegesis of the poem in *Olson's Push* (Baton Rouge, La.: Louisiana State University Press, 1978), pp. 9–29.

9. Charles Olson, *A Bibliography on America for Ed Dorn* (San Francisco: Four Seasons Foundation, 1964), pp. 6, 15.

10. Brooks Adams, *The Law of Civilization and Decay: An Essay on History* (New York: Knopf, 1948), p. 61.

11. Carl G. Jung, *The Integration of the personality*, trans. Stanley Dell (New York: Farrar and Rinehart, 1939), p. 76.

12. The term is Creeley's. See his "Preface to the First Edition" of *ML*, 6.

13. Brooks Adams, *The New Empire* (New York: Macmillan Co., 1902), pp. xiv–xv.

14. Quoted from Frank Cole Babbitt's introduction to "The E at Delphi," in *Plutarch's Moralia*, trans. Frank Cole Babbitt, The Loeb Classical Library, 14 vols. (Cambridge, Mass.: Harvard University Press, 1936), 5:194.

15. Ibid., p. 192.

16. Ibid.

17. J. B. Philip, "Charles Olson Reconsidered," *Journal of American Studies* 5 (Dec. 1971): 303–4.

18. Adams, *The New Empire*, p. 38.

19. "The priests seem invariably to have worn their hair matted with the blood of the sacrificial victims" (Thompson, *Civilization of the Mayas*, p. 76).

20. "It is not improbable that the governing priest class was overthrown by a revolt of the masses. . . . With the expulsion or death of the ruler-priest class the peasants reverted to the simple agricultural religion most suited to their needs, gradually losing at the same time the knowledge of how to produce delicately painted pottery and well-executed sculpture in stone" (ibid., pp. 15–16).

21. Norbert Wiener, *Cybernetics; or, Control and Communication in the Animal and the Machine*, 2d ed. (1948; reprint ed., New York: M.I.T. Press, 1961).

22. Norbert Wiener, *The Human Use of Human Beings: Cybernetics and Society* (Boston: Houghton Mifflin Co., 1950), p. 71.

23. "The message is a discrete or continuous sequence of measurable events distributed in time" (Wiener, *Cybernetics*, p. 8).

24. *Plutarch's Moralia*, p. 192.

25. "I do go in circles, in fact believe that only if one does does one finally suck up the vertu in anything. I am not aware that we proceed in straight lines at all" (*SVH*, p. 35).

26. Thompson, *Civilization of the Mayas*, p. 14.

27. Ernest Fenollosa, *The Chinese Written Character as a Medium for Poetry*, ed. Ezra Pound (San Francisco: City Lights Books, 1936), p. 33.

28. "and when a people are so disposed, it should come as no surprise that, long before any of these accomplishments, the same people [the Maya] did an improvement on nature—the domestication of maize—which remains one of the world's wonders, even to a nation of Burbanks" ("The Human Universe," *HU*, 7).

29. Olson wrote to Creeley, "Point (2) above, as VIOLENCE—killing, the heart, out, etc: those sons of bitches, those 'scholars'—how they've cut that story out, to make the Mayan palatable to their fucking selves, foundations, & tourists!" (*ML*, p. 23).

30. Heraclitus, "Fragment 99," trans. Philip Wheelwright, in *Heraclitus* (Princeton, N.J.: Princeton University Press, 1959), p. 90. Actually as Davenport observes (p. 258), Olson paraphrases Shakespeare's Timon here:

> Thy mistress is o' the brothel! Son of sixteen.
> Pluck the lined crutch from they old limping sire,
> With it beat out his brains! Piety and fear,
> Religion to the gods, peace, justice, truth.
> Domestic awe, night-rest, and neighborhood,
> Instruction, manners, mysteries and trades,
> Degrees, observances, customs and laws,
> Decline to your confounding contraries.

> (4.1.13–20)

31. Rosenthal finds the line, "I am no Greek, hath not th'advantage," "emptily tricky . . . memorable for its weak grammar . . . [and] functionally indefensible" (Rosenthal, *The New Poets*, p. 165), but I think it may be "tricky" in a fuller, ironical sense. The grammatical violation is, after all, a demonstrated contempt for the rigidities of "discourse," and in its way complements the sarcastic flippancy of the word "advantage."

32. Robert von Hallberg, "Olson's Relation to Pound and Williams," *Contemporary Literature* 15 (Winter 1974): 42.

33. Charles Olson, "Memorial Letter," *Origin*, no. 20 (January 1971): 47.

34. Olson's lecture, Black Mountain College, 1956: "I am the more persuaded of the importance and use of Whitehead's thought that I did not know his work . . . until last year" (Charters, *Olson/Melville* p. 84).

35. Alfred North Whitehead, *Process and Reality* (New York: Macmillan Co., 1929), pp. 514–15.
36. *Plutarch's Moralia*, pp. 191–93.

4

The Distances

> Man is estranged from that with which
> he is most familiar.
> > —Heraclitus

The poems that make up *The Distances* are variations on a single theme. This is what gives this first major collection of Olson's work its integrity. "The Kingfishers," which opens the selection, has already exposed us to one evocation of that theme: a sense of loss, separation—of "distances" that intrude between us and our direct experience of reality. "Man is estranged from that with which he is most familiar" is the Heraclitean diagnosis that Olson seeks to record in this poem and those which follow. Even the acidly satiric broadside, "Letter for Melville 1951," funnels its final rage at the root cause of that estrangement: "discourse" and the academic discourse-mongers who alienate us from our familiarity with Melville's genius. At "the Melville Society's 'One Hundredth Birthday Party' for MOBY-DICK," Olson warns,

> . . . you will have to hear one very bright man speak,
> > so bright
> he'll sound so good that every one of you will think
> he knows whereof he speaks, he'll say such forward
> > things, he'll tag
> the deific principle in nature, the heroic
> principle in man, he'll spell
> what you do not have such time to read as he
> such definitions so denotatively clear you'll think
> > you'll understand
> (discourse is such a lie) that
> > Herman Melville
> was no professional . . .

> > > > > (*D*, 52)

There is he in academic regalia: the heinous intermediary, the purveyor of logical simplification, the Anti-Herodotus who obviates "finding out for one's self," the manufacturer of "distances," the personification of "discourse."

In many of the poems, however, hostility to "discourse" is not so directly expressed. It often comes in bewildering forms. "The Praises," for example, thematically echoes "The Kingfishers" in lamenting a loss of value that results when a healthy "will to cohere" (*HU*, 21) yields to the corrosive consequences of "dispersion":

> What has been lost
> is the secret of secrecy, is
> the value, viz., that the work get done, and quickly,
> without the loss of due and profound respect for
> the materials
>
> which is not so easy as it sounds, nor
> can it permit the dispersion which follows from
> too many having too little
> knowledge
>
> (*D*, 25)

In "The Kingfishers" the "secret" of coherency had been sought in the Mayan ruins; in "the Praises" it is stalked within the mysteries of the Pythagorean Brotherhood. Although the theme of the poem differs little from the position Olson expressed in his essay "The Gate and the Center," its conduct at first seems impenetrable, and its demands upon the reader prodigious.

The materials that make it up include such precious items as: the Pythagorean "secret" of the dodecahedron and an account of Hippasus's impiety in divulging it, a description of the destructive fire at Metapontum in which the followers of Pythagoras perished, the Fibonacci number sequence, the four epiphanies of the neo-Platonist Ammonius, a quotation from the notebook of da Vinci, a number of allusions to Plutarch's "The E at Delphi," and even some paraphrased bathroom graffiti. Although these items seem presented historically, no heed is paid to chronology, and the poem is broken periodically by apparent non-sequitur. No less than with "The Kingfishers" the customary methods of explication seem not merely ineffective but somehow irrelevant. How do we proceed?

The title seems a good beginning. It is extracted from a response by Ammonius in Plutarch's essay to an almost exhaustive examination by the other symposiasts of the number five as the underlying reality of the universe. Although Ammonius appreciates their ingenuity, he cautiously points out that

> it is not worthwhile to argue too precisely over these matters with the young, except to say that everyone of the numbers will provide not a little for them that wish to sing its praises.[1]

Olson was probably attracted by Ammonius's cautious skepticism—his appreciation of the vulnerability of reason to the lure of single explanations for things as a discursive defense against the "difficulties" that characterize one's actual experience of the "familiar." To demonstrate the limitations of reason, Olson offers his own examination of the number five. He points out first how the "Master" (Pythagoras) deduced from the fact that there are "five solid figures" that the "Sphere of the Universe arose from / the dodecahedron." Thus *five* attained virtually religious status within the Pythagorean Brotherhood and was regarded as a divine secret. *Five*'s supernatural potency, the poem points out, was demonstrated by Antiochus's victory over the Galates, who were routed by the mere display of a pentagraph.

He concedes that the remarkable powers of *five* are visible in the Fibonacci number sequence (1, 1, 2, 3, 5, 8, 13, 21, . . .) in which each term is the sum of the two preceding terms. When two diagonals of a pentagon intersect, the ratio of the lengths of the two segments is the same as the ratio of two consecutive numbers of a Fibonacci sequence. The poem notes further that Fibonacci ratios extend to horticulture:

the ratios 5/8, 8/13
in the seed-cones of fir-trees,
the ratio 21/34
in normal daisies . . .

Even zoology yields to the dominance of *five*: "Pendac-
tylism is general in the animal kingdom." Indeed, this
dominance (the "law of phi") appears to proceed
"asymptotically toward graphic and tangible."
    While all this demonstrable evidence for the universal
applicability of *five* may warm the heart of a rationalist, for
Olson it threatened to accomplish what he elsewhere
warned was what the "rational" always wants:

> to seek one explanation—or to put it more evenly, undo
> the paradox (the rational mind hates the familiar, and
> has to make it ordinary by explaining it, in order not to
> experience it).[*SVH*, 31]

The relentless epistemological tyranny of *five* endangers
paradoxical mystery and renders the universe "ordinary"
through discursive, explanatory reduction. The "law of
phi" denies man the experience of the "familiar" and effects his eventual incarceration in a "universe of discourse." As if to frustrate the advance of this menace.
Olson unveils conflicting evidence: "crystals . . . lilies
tulips   the hyacinth." These nonpentagonal items are de-
putized as guardians of the fragile, mysterious allure of
"woman," and the sudden objection, "o, that's not fair,"
comes as a natural, human revulsion against a rationally
reduced world that would deny such pleasures:

> let
> woman keep her jewels, odd man
> his pleasure of her glow, . . .

As the poem continues, Olson again enlists the support
of Ammonius by citing that philosopher's admirable alternative to the "law of phi":

what is related must remain enigmatic

Enigma, in other words, is a more satisfactory "glue" to hold the universe together than the number five. This appeal to Ammonius's epiphanies establishes a world that proceeds in the fashion of *enantiodromia*, that is, in the conflict of opposites. *Fives* appropriately coexist with *fours*, and *sixes* properly conflict with *sevens*. This is the "irrational" "secret of secrecy" that Ammonius insists must be kept from the "brutish," who, presumably, lack the capability to seek the truth that lies beyond logic.

Ammonius's unabashed elitism helps us to understand Olson's otherwise confusing stance in the midst of the epistemological options he arranges about himself. His "praises" celebrate no single number, no specific sign, nor even a divine principle that might unlock the mysteries of the universe. His scorn for such is apparent:

> You would have a sign. Look:
> to fly? a fly can do that;
> to try the moon? a moth
> as well; to walk on water? a straw
> precedes you

No, Olson's "praises" are reserved for "the secret of secrecy" itself. This notion is defined by his account of the fall of the Pythagorean Brotherhood. Hippasus is the villain, for he was

> the first to publish (write down, divulge)
> the secret,
> the construction of, from 12 pentagons,
> the sphere
> "Thus was he punished for his impiety"

Hippasus's villainy, however, was not the disclosure of the specific construction of the dodecahedron but the betrayal of the Brotherhood's "containment" (*D*, 26)—that is, its "will to cohere." The consequence of his act was the "dispersion" of "too little / knowledge" to "too many" (*D*, 25). Behind the *apparent* rationality of the Brotherhood lay its secret acknowledgement of irrational numbers, and commentators frequently assign the disclosure of this fact to Hippasus as well as his revelation of the dodecahedron. Thus, the Pythagorean number divinity rested on a foundation of irrational enigma, a truth that could accommodate only these cultural elite "OF THEBES" who are "active, enjoy thought," and are "LESKENOI" (*D*, 24).

Hippasus's betrayal prefigures the "mob" that so effectively "disperses" the Pythagorean "containment" at Metapontum, but it is important to appreciate that even though the dispersion of the "secret of secrecy" caused the political downfall of the Brotherhood, its "secret" does not completely perish in the fire. Two survivors, Philalaos and Lysis, withstand the disaster and carry the "secret" forward to Plato. These cultural elite (later Olson would dub them "polis"), by their work and the use to which it would be put, sustain the "containment." They carry the banner, so to speak, of Pythagorean "polis" and illuminate the enigma of the poem's opening line. Surely the half-burned "She" whose "body skipped out of death" is none other than the indomitable "secret of secrecy" that managed to evade extinction at Metapontum through the containment, the work, and the "USE" of Philalaos and Lysis.

The "present inquiry" (*D*, 24) that "The Praises" undertakes finally evolves into a series of hygienic imperatives:

> Avert, avert, avoid
> pollution, to be clean
> in a dirty time
> (*D*, 24)

An appeal is raised to "Wheel" for assistance in this cleansing:

> O Wheel, aid us
> to get the gurry off

The "pollution" that Olson has in mind is clearly the kind of epistemological "sprawl" he describes as the opposite of "objectism" in "Projective Verse." There he associates "sprawling" with a commitment to "artificial forms out-side" man's nature, and recommends instead that "if he is contained within his nature ... he is participant in the larger force" (*HU*, 60). Thus, the "dispersion" of knowl-edge is tantamount to a surrender to "discourse" and, ac-cordingly, "pollution" is merely another synonym for "mu-sick" (*M*, 3), "pejorocracy" (*M*, 3, 6, 73), and clas-sificatory logic. The "Wheel," which is petitioned to "draw" the "truth" that signs are impotent "to my house," must be the "god, converter, discloser" who "will answer, / will look out, if you will look, look!" (*D*, 25). This "god," however, is no conventional diety; he sits enthroned in "that mere pea of bone / where the axes meet, cross-roads of the system." He is a divine pineal gland that, consistent with Olson's proprioceptive convictions (*AP*, 17–21), synthesizes the body and mind of man. interestingly, the *Encyclopaedia Britannica*, a frequent Olson source, notes that

> the Pythagorean Brotherhood had ... much in common with the Orphic communities which sought by rites and abstinences to purify the believer's soul and enable it to escape from "The Wheel of Birth."

If it is to this Wheel that Olson alludes (or, just as plausibly, to Jung's center and circumference of the Self), his inten-tion was precisely the opposite of that of the Orphic com-munities. Rather than "escape" from the Wheel's con-straints, Olson recommends commitment to its purifying physicality. The Wheel is resolutely a gland, not a soul; a gland, moreover, that adequately functions as god and dis-closer. From its secure, biological foundation man finds the proper vantage from which to "look," and what he sees, of course, are not the specters of discourse but the "purifying" lineaments of the "familiar."

The "familiar" is a pre-Socratic phenomenon and "The Praises" and "The Kingfishers" both energetically press the theme (which is the theme of *the Distances* as a whole) that man can achieve an enormous gain by a return to that time, anterior to "Greek" epistemology, when thought and action, mind and body, logos and speech resisted division and cohered in the unity of the "familiar." Perhaps as a didactic courtesy, Olson wedges between these two companion poems three Poundian gestures that seem to indicate his having taken to heart the master's view that "the first credential we should demand of a critic is *his* ideograph of the good; of what he considers valid writing."[2] They are "ABCs," "ABCs (2)," and "ABCs (3—for Rimbaud)."

The "ABC" trio does serve as Olson's "ideograph of the good," particularly in the way it defines his stance in relation to contemporary friends and foes—specifically, Eliot, Pound, and Williams. Its most interesting point, however, has to do with a kind of language purification Olson referred to as "nominalization." Parmenides of Elea, Creeley helpfully observes, is a pre-Socratic illustration of the nominalization principle:

> The thing that can be thought and that for the sake of which the thought exists is the same; for you cannot find thought without something that is, as to which it is uttered.[3]

As an example of Olson's Parmenidean persuasion on the issue, Creeley cites a passage from "Tyrian Businesses" in *The Maximus Poems*:

> There may be no more names than there are objects
> There can be no more verbs than there are
> actions . . .
>
> (*M*, 36)

This is no simple program of word rationing; it is a method for finding in root nouns their connection to primordial cosmic truths inherent in them. "I'm buggy on . . . the Proper Noun," he wrote to Elaine Feinstein,

> so much so I wld take it Pun is Rime, all from tope/ type/trope, that built in is the connection, in each of us,

> to Cosmos, and if one taps, via psyche, plus a "true"
> adherence of Muse, one does reveal "Form." (*HU*, 97)

The idea is to recover the roots of nouns so that their cosmic connections may be tapped. Nouns are "magical," Olson contends, in that "the naming character already in the noun, inherent to it, original with its even existing . . . is in the word no matter who uses it."[4]

Access to the original, inherent "naming character" of a noun is through one's individual psyche, presumably deep within the Collective Unconscious. Thus, in "ABCs" we learn that the "acquisition" of "Speech [takes] . . . as long / as I am old" (*D*, 12). Speech, unlike cosmically disconnected discourse, reveals its primordial meaning to the user through vivid particular experience. Thus,

> rat   on the first floor landing of the three-decker
>   (grey)
> black   eat a peck of storage batteries 'fore
>   I die
> cabbage   my friend Cabbage, with whom to bake
>   potatoes up Fisher's Hill
> rust   in the bed of Beaver Brook—from the junk in it
>   And the iris ("flags" we called 'em)
>   And the turtle I was surprised by
>
> (*D*, 12)

Finding a local habitation for every name may indeed discover a collective root meaning discernible by virtue of our collective connections with the cosmos; for those with less confidence in a Collective Unconscious, however, it may seem perilously like private language. "ABCs (2)," for example, ends:

> And the boat,
> how he swerves it to avoid the yelping rocks
> where the tidal river rushes
>
> (*D*, 14)

This passage has no apparent connection with the poem it closes, which discusses how the stance of "objectism" can avail one of the wisdom of the Collective Unconscious "coiled or unflown / in the marrow of the bone," and when the boat abruptly "swerves" into the poem, the reader literally finds himself at sea. The "swerving" boat has no reference for him.

It does for Olson, however, and it graphically illustrates how "localized" his language is to private experiences. Olson's connection between the swerving boat and the rest of his poem can be discovered in a 1956 lecture at Black Mountain in which he reminisces about the circumstances under which he first reached an understanding of myth:

> I remember exactly the place and hour of my first attempt to write down how I understood myth to be—on the Annisquam River, winter, 1939, with Schwartz's mother-in-law, in whom I took great phantasy pleasure, in the same house![5]

He than goes on in the lecture to develop the story of how his book *Call Me Ishmael* matured in his thought processes from rhythm to image to knowing and finally to construct. Here, however, he interrupts himself with this abrupt return to particular circumstances:

> (And the boat did swerve then, just because Schwartz's mother-in-law and I and all my people were, even then, involved in avoiding the
> yelping rocks
> where the tidal river rushes.

Olson *privately* links, we see, "myth" as well as the "objectism" involved in the writing of *Call Me Ishmael* with Schwartz's mother-in-law, the "swerving boat," and the tidal river. It may be overestimating the "magic" of nominalization to assume the reader can make a connection with the cosmos through these same particulars.

Nevertheless, it is Olson's claim that "man as common has to be restored by way of you or me *as particular* [italics added]," and in order to "accomplish the common" through particulars, there are "two attacks":

> A. *the proper nominative* (exact particular specific anec-
> dote explored into universe by conjecture... or B. *the
> erasure of* the proper nominative ... (the erasure, that is,
> only of the names, but a retention of the force of the
> common by no falling for realism, or the false par-
> ticularism of the "autobiographical"—that because it
> happens to me, it is therefore going to be of significance
> to others. (*LO*, 82)

The "swerving boat" in "ABCs (2)" is obviously an instance
of "attack B," in which the proper nominative "Schwartz"
is "erased" from the poem while the remaining particulars
("the yelping rocks / where the tidal river rushes") are retained to assure the "force of the common." We may detect
the operation of "attack A" in "The Praises" where both
"exact specific anecdote" *and* proper names are utilized.

The "false particularism" of Pound, Eliot, and, especially, Williams provokes Olson's irritation in "ABCs
(3—for Rimbaud)":

> Or watching of, the Passaic of
> orange peels? Cats
> win in urbe, NOT
> usura or those queer long white (like finger bandages
> balloons? The dyes
> of realism?
>
> (*D*, 15)

Williams's *Paterson*, apparently, has fallen "for realism"
and the deliberate pun "dyes" leaves no mistake possible
that as far as Olson is concerned realism as a methodology
is dead.

In its place, as a practical remedy for stopping the "mu-
sick" and restoring "speech-force" to a language suffering
the anemia of discourse, Olson suggests syllables:

> Is it any more than
> a matter of syllables?
> (*D*, 16)

Perhaps not, but a program that is determined to "accomplish the common," restore "speech-force," avert "false particularism," and clear the air of "mu-sick" must place its faith in very special syllables indeed. Olson's point, as is often the case, finds clarification in "Projective Verse":

> In any given instance, because there is a choice
> of words,
> the choice, if a man is in there, will be
> spontaneously,
> the obedience of his ear to the syllables.
>
> (*HU*, 53)

The poet spontaneously "accomplishes the common" by remaining illogically obedient to his syllable-sensitive ear, for "it is from the union of the mind and the ear that the syllable is born" (*HU*, 54). The process is "swift as synapse" (*D*, 12) and takes the poet magically to the root of the nominative where he discovers:

> what we do not know of ourselves
> of who they are who lie
> coiled or unflown
> in the marrow of the bone
>
> (*D*, 14)

Nominalization is a tool for gaining access to those primordial others who make up the collective unconscious. Nouns can probe the bone marrow and discover grounds for truth far beyond the ego; nouns can reach "man as common."

Two historical poems in *The Distances*, "There was a Youth Named Thomas Granger" (*D*, 17–19) and "At Yorktown" (*D*, 20–21), illustrate how the proper nominative as "exact particular specific anecdote explored into universe by conjecture" can transform simple past fact into contemporarily relevant, mythic reenactment. Truth in any absolute sense is beyond historical resuscitation by language, and so Olson unabashedly announces that "there is truth, in one sense only, that, you are it if you make yrself clear" (*LO*, 83).

How Olson "clarifies" himself through *Bradford's History "Of Plimouth Plantation"* [6] is a testament not only to his formal ability to change a "prose source into poetry by adjusting rhythm," [7] but an illustration of the commonality of "particular specific anecdote." The first poem lifts the evidence of Thomas Granger's sodomy trial almost verbatim from its source in Bradford, but it is clear from the start that the historical event as past fact is not the poem's concern at all. Granger's trial is not cited as an act done but as an act men do in common. Thomas Granger is a timeless figure in a ritual reenactment. The poem performatively combines the doing with the telling.

Olson marshals the evidence that makes up his poem in a way that underscores his familiar concerns. The anomaly of Bradford's comparison of sin to the natural flow of a river is a piece of *ironie trouvée*:

> As it is with waters when
> their streames are stopped or damed up, wickednes
> ... searches every wher it get vente ...

The laws and the authorities that exact those laws are likened to dams that vainly attempt to block the natural process of nature. Mr. Bradford, who "forbear[s] perticulers," is persuaded of Granger's guilt by theological abstractions gleaned from "Luther, Calvin, Hen: Bulin:. Theo: Beza. Zanch." The ultimate affront of the event, however, is the particularized waste that intervening law exacts:

> A very sade spectakle it was; for first the mare,
> and then ye cowe, and ye rest of ye lesser catle,
> wer kild before his face, according to ye law
> Levit: 20:15.
> and then he him selfe
>   and no use made of any part of them

The tyranny of abstractions over the useful "familiar" items of the natural process is the sad rite that "Thomas

Granger" reenacts, but history itself can be an abstract ty-
rant, too, if it is not understood as contemporary event.
"At Yorktown" is even more overt in its repudiation of the
pastness of the past. It presents a contrast of a vividly present, mythically alive Yorktown where

> the long dead
> loosen the earth, heels
> sink in, over an abatis
> a bird wheels . . .

with its dead historical forebear:

> at York-town only the flies
> dawdle, like history,
> in the sun

"Yorktown" vies with "York-town" for contemporary relevance and of course only the former can prevail, for as
past mythically ritualized in present, Yorktown's artifacts
do not gather flies as they dawdle in the sun but forcefully
"scream / without noise / like a gull" (*D*, 21).

"At Yorktown" and "Thomas Granger" are formal il-
lustrations of "attack A" in the strategy of nominalization
in that both exploit "exact particular specific anecdote" for
the purpose of mythic reenactment. In explaining "attack
B" (the *erasure of* the proper nominative") to Cid Corman,
Olson warned that the tactic "involved altogether fresh devices of time, of juxtaposition: in fact, has to be solved literally in Non-Euclidean & Geometrical SPACE-TIME
ways" (*LO*, 82).

"In Cold Hell, In Thicket" (*D*, 27–32), an obscurely
moving poem, is a non-Euclidean experiment in that it
boldly celebrates what Olson once called "the whole seis-
matic shift in men's attentions" or "the return to space."[8] It
achieves this non-Euclidean goal by means of "erasure of
the proper nominative"; it is a sustained application of
"attack B."

Cold hell is the epistemological climate that the nonprojective man finds himself suffering as he just begins to
feel the impact of the "return to space." He finds himself

imprisoned in a thicket of obsolete "attentions" that still
impinge on him by dint of their "strong," "abstract," "cold"
authority. He endures a state of transitional despair in
which

> All things are made bitter, words even
> are made to taste like paper, wars get tossed up
> like lead soldiers used to be
> (in a child's attic) lined up
> to be knocked down, as I am,
> by firings from a spit-hardened fort, fronted
> as we are, here, from where we must go
>
> (D, 27)

The "lead soldiers" in the "child's attic" and the "spit-
hardened fort," although "erased" of proper nomination,
are autobiographical items that appear in *Stocking Cap*.[9]
There they function as reminiscence but here they are intended to evoke some common awareness of distance or
separation from that which is familiar and real. These
items possess the vicariousness of all discourse. They mark
the distance that separates spontaneous act from "thought
about act," vivid experience from expression of experience, and vital myth from historical report. Words taste
like paper because they have lost speech-force. Wars are
like toy soldiers that are knocked down in pretend skir-
mishes because they meet us as abstractions rather than as
brutal, head-on carnages. Even the protagonist confesses
that he is "knocked down" by firings from that "spit-
hardened fort," the fort itself being a kind of citadel of
"discourse" that has been hardened by convention.

Is "cold hell" endurable? "[C]an a man stay (can men)
confronted / thus?" Is a "return to space" a viable option?
Olson's faith is that for a man "there is always / a thing he
can do" (D, 27) even though

> In hell it is not easy
> to know the traceries, the markings
> (the canals, the pits, the mountings by which space
> declares herself . . .

Space declares and demands from those who would choose it a "redistribution of value, will & mind," for

> Space is the mark of new history, and the measure of work now afoot is the depth of the perception of space, both as space informs objects and as it contains, in antithesis to time, secrets of a humanitas eased out of contemporary narrows.[10]

As a kind of mythic evocation of these "secrets," Olson employs the legend of Geb, the Egyptian god of the earth, and his sister-wife, Nut, whom the poem designates as the "necessary goddess" (*D*, 28) of space. The monarchical "ease" that Geb enjoys, as he lies "in stasis under her, his sister, [with] awkward stars drawn for teats to pleasure him," is contrasted to the "reluctant, imageless, unpleasured" *un*ease of the poem's speaker, who is mired in cold hell. The thicket is his prison. Branches and snowflakes guarantee his unprivileged discomfort. Their "black and silvered knivings," like imprints of typeface, are "awkwardnesses" that are "already done" (*D*, 28); they are the prison bars of a discourse solidly rooted in convention rather than space-time. Discourse is the cause of the unease of cold hell and so the speaker's urgent appeal is:

> How can he change . . . these awkwardnesses?
> . . .
> How can he make . . .
> a vessel fit for moving?
> How can he make out . . .
> of this low eye-view,
> size?
>
> (*D*, 28)

The problem is to transform the constraining linguistic thicket into a grammar of ease so that the "low-eye view" might be raised sufficiently to see the "traceries" and "markings" of space. In achieving this elevated perspective, through what can only be called a projective liberation from discourse, man is restored his original, primordial "size."

The word "size" has special meaning for Olson. It is no mere metaphor to describe a poet's achievement of epic scope, but an anthropological claim that Olson first suggested in "The Gate and the Center":

> I have this dream, that just as we cannot now see & say the size of these early HUMAN KINGS [the Sumerians], we cannot, by the very lost token of their science, see what size man can be once more capable of, once the turn of the flow of his energies that I speak of as the WILL TO COHERE is admitted, and its energy taken up. (*HU*, 21)

The cold hell of discourse has literally cut man down to size. It has caused a loss of speech-force—a linguistic anemia—which has severed man from nature's energies. "We have been shocked," Olson adds,

> at what we did not know nature's energies capable of . . . energy is larger than man, but therefore, if he taps it as it is in himself, his uses of himself are EXTENSIBLE in human directions & degree not recently granted.

Geb and Nut, then, are primordial poets who illustrate a mythic "size" potentially available to men. Their projective skills enable them to achieve "archings traced and picked enough to hold / to stay" (*D*, 28) and they stand as the projective ideal for man who as yet remains frozen in his cold hell,

>   not daring
> where the grass grows, to move his feet from fear
> he'll trespass on his own dissolving bones, here
> where there is altogether too much remembrance
>   (*D*, 28–29)

The dread of trespassing on "dissolving bones" and the awareness that "too much remembrance" suffuses the thicket underscore the point that cold hell is a consequence of an obsession with time. Time riddenness is the psychological equivalent of the thicket's restraining branches that keep the speaker from the freedom of the "open field" ("where the grass grows"). In bondage to history and thus cut off from the freedom of *'istorin*, he is coldly earthbound without spatial awareness.

The "unease" of cold hell at least provokes anthropological speculation: "Who / am I?" (*D*, 29). The reply is terse and deceptively barren: a "fix" and a "particle" within a "congery of particles carefully picked one by another" (*D*, 29). This starkly scientific account is quickly clothed by a simile:

> as in this thicket, each
> smallest branch, plant, fern, root . . .
> must now . . . be
> isolated, observed, picked over, measured, raised
> as though a word, an accuracy were a pincer!

Bleak as man's awareness of his spatial identity may seem with its ego-deflating reductionism, Olson nevertheless counts it as one of the "*gains* of space," for as "fix," as "particle" among particles, man wins citizenship in the universe of objectism:

> Man as object is equatable to all other nature, is neutron, is on the one hand thus no more than a tree or pitch-blende but is, therefore, returned to an abiding place, the primordial, where he can rest again as he did once with less knowledge to confirm his *humilitas*.[11]

Although space is a primordial "abiding place" to which man returns with humility, his homecoming is not easily effected. The loss of ego that the goddess of space demands renders the "taste" of her "bitter" (*D*, 29). Indeed, spatial humility means a reorientation as radical as religious regeneration. "Man as object in space as against man as subject of time," Olson argues, "makes possible a life-death concept which admits man's reflection as force in nature."[12] As force, man ceases to be an entity defined as ego and becomes instead a spatial energy perceived only through "traceries" and "fixes" (things done) like electrons in a cloud chamber.

The courage required to humiliate the ego and commit to space is so great (" . . . who / can turn this total thing, invert / and let the ragged sleeves be seen / by any bitch or common character?" [D, 30]) that the hell-imprisoned hero cannot bring himself to move. The challenge is frightening, and this is

> why
> he stands so awkward where he is, why
> his feet are held, like some ragged crane's

No outside force or deity consigns him to his cold hell or his imagined paradise, for

> man, men, are now their own wood
> and thus their own hell and paradise

Moreover, man is obedient. He is "something to be wrought, to be shaped, to be carved, for use, for / others" (D, 31), even though this

> does not in the least lessen his, this unhappy man's
> obscurities, his
> confrontations

His destiny is to be ever "moving off / into the soil, on to his own bones," crossing the "field" that "is not a choice" but is "as dangerous as a prayer, as a death." The difference from cold hell is that here the world has been returned to him; space has restored him a "human universe" in which he journeys as through a "wilderness," obediently following a "demand" (D, 32).

Like "In Cold Hell, In Thicket," "The Moon Is the Number 18" is a poem energized by grief. It is, in fact, an elegy occasioned by the death of Olson's mother, but as is usually the case, the poet's energetic concerns pulsate far beyond that funereal fact. The machinery of the poem is supplied by the moon card of the tarot pack, number

XVIII of the major arcana. A block print of the card, designed by Olson with the help of Corrado Cagli, accompanied the poem in its initial publication in Origin 1 (Spring 1951). The arcanum depicts a moon surrounded by sharp rays (resembling, as the poem notes, a monstrance) dripping blood or dew. Two towers stand in the background, and a path, a stream, howling dogs, and a crayfish or crab arising from a lake complete the scene. In some representations a man sits with a dog at his feet making music to a woman who stands on the balcony of one of the towers.

The poem invites symbolic analysis of the sort provided by Richard G. Ingber, who traces a number of potential allusions to occult, Christian, and hermetic sources, relying a bit heavily on such tenuous links as the fact that the German word for dew, *Tau*, has a synonym that means "rope," and that the Greek *tau* can be equated with the Cross.[13] True, Olson's etymological fascination with the roots of words lends some plausibility to Ingber's explication and Olson's familiarity with the symbolic idiom of the tarot cards is unquestioned; nevertheless, such a symbolic analysis is so counter to the kinetic spirit of Olson's poetics that it must be viewed with suspicion.

Another approach would be to relate the poem's energies and objects to those ubiquitous concerns that supply Olson's work as a whole with its integrity. For example, the atmosphere of the poem suggests the same sense of loss as that of "In Cold Hell, In Thicket." Some element that once integrated experience is missing: in the case of this poem, the mysterious "she" who formerly sat in the "red tower" where now the "grieving son" sits

> alone with cat & crab
> and sound is, is, his
> conjecture
> (*D*, 34)

The tower, and what formerly and presently inhabits it, is

> where what triumph there is, is: there
> is all substance, all creature

>   all there is against the dirty moon, against
>   number, image, sortilege

The battle lines are clear. The son, the baying "blue dogs," "she," "the cat & crab, / and sound" and finally, the "grieving" son's "conjecture" are all pitted against the moon that "has no air."

The tower is an archetypal battered bastion manned by a mere garrison force bereft of "she." Nevertheless, it is a fortress that defends "all substance, all creature," the animus of the baying dogs, the motion of the crab and (perhaps most important) the "air" or breath that the moon lacks. The tarot tower resembles unmistakably the house of "animal man" that Olson describes in "The Resistance":

> the house he [man] is, this house that moves, breathes, acts, this house where his life is, where he dwells against the enemy, against the beast.
>   Or the fraud. This organism now our citadel never was cathedral, draughty tenement of soul, was what it is ground, stone, wall, cannon, tower. In this intricate structure are we based, now more certainly than ever (beseiged, overthrown), for its power is bone muscle nerve blood brain a man . . . (*HU*, 47–48)

The tower, as the citadel of physical man, is a *potential* human universe. In it the "preening" cat of the intellect "watches," while the proprioceptive crab "moves." Both are "attentive . . . to catch / human sound" that, when it presumably is quickened by breath, becomes the grieving son's "conjecture."

The poem is indeed a "monstrance" that holds not only the complex grief of a son mourning the loss of his mother but also the grief of man bereft of that with which he is most familiar—his own organism.

When Olson proposed to Corman that *Origin* devote fifty pages to "the shifting correspondence of two writers" (*LO*, 13), he conceived of it as "an immense business . . . an intimate, moving, upshooting thing." The idea never quite materialized, but Olson's faith in such an epistolary form

never flagged. In *The Distances* there is at least one dis-
juncted experiment of correspondence as itself an open,
poetic form: "To Gerhardt, there, among Europe's things
of which he has written us in his 'Brief an Creeley und
Olson.'" In its original appearance in *Origin #4*,[14] the
poem had the advantage of its companion piece by Rainer
Maria Gerhardt, the brilliant young German editor of
Fragmente (a little magazine published in Freiburg, Germany), in translated form ("Letter for Creeley and
Olson").

Gerhardt's letter-poem is a kind of tribute to projectivist
poetics, composed in six sections he calls "montages." It
owes its suffused theme essentially to the kind of notions
Olson had probed in "The Gate and the Center":

> ... anyone who wants to begin to get straight has to, to
> start ... to uneducate himself first ... to get back in
> order to get on. ...

> ... all Indo-European language (ours) appears to stem
> from the very same ground on which the original
> agglutinative language was invented, Sumeria ... and
> that our language can be seen to hold in itself now as
> many of these earliest elements as it does Sanskrit
> roots. ...

> the poet is the only pedagogue left, to be trusted. ...
> We are only just beginning to gauge the backward of lit-
> erature, breaking through the notion that Greece began
> it, to the writings farther back to the Phoenicians, to the
> Babylonians, behind them the Akkadians, and, most
> powerful of all, the Sumerian poets, the first makers,
> better than 2000 years prior to Homer, Hesiod &
> Herodotus. (*HU*, 17)

Thus, Gerhardt, in assessing the cultural status of Europe,
writes:

> Ishtar endures
> the land is bright with the Greeks

He hopes to break the Greek stranglehold through the
presumed power of his Laurentian "litany of Europe's

places" (D, 37) that in "one unique upheaval of one continent" may effect a genuine "returning home." Heeding Olson's appeal that we must look backward, he traces the "black bough" of Europe's Sumerian and Assyrian cultural heritage that he is certain underlies the Greek "brightness." He documents the Hellenization of Tammuz, Enlil, Tamar, and Ereb until eventually he feels justified in paraphrasing Pound's "Mauberley":

> having lost the tragic pose
> the air only for us
>   the breath
>
> of rot
>   smiling at the good mouth
>   for two gross of broken statues
>   for a few thousand battered books

Gerhardt's remedy for this "breath of rot" is typically Olsonian: a journey backward. Specifically, he recommends that we "go home" with a

> passport to America
> via the Punjab and Indus valley in the tracks
>   of poets
>   of language

In more practical language this means:

> in old Europe
> translate Pound
>   and Williams
>   attempt
> these vocable in a way
>   still unknown here . . .
> old Gaul
>   young in years
> an oldyoung nag   broken in
>   many languages in
> the still stubborn thing
>   grab it by the tail Olson

One would think that Olson would be flattered by the obvious adulation of his European disciple, and, in his own peculiar way, he was. In his funeral poem for Gerhardt, "The Death of Europe," he acknowledges how Rainer "gave us all hearing / in Germany" and how he was "the first of Europe / I could have words with" (*D*, 64, 65). And yet in his reply to Gerhardt's letter there is a note of the wary dogmatist who is nervous about the young upstart who threatens to move in on his territory just a little bit too boldly. In some passages Olson is clearly putting Gerhardt in his place. Commenting on Gerhardt's litany of European cities, for example, Olson chides

> Or from the other side of time, from a time on the other
>   side of yourself
> from which you have so lightly borrowed men,
>   naming them
>   as though,
> like your litany of Europe's places, you could take up
> their power: magic, my light-fingered faust,
> is not so easily sympathetic.
>
>   (*D*, 37)

Olson's pique is over Gerhardt's improper use of nominalization. Mere naming will not conjure the primordial energies. One must be archetypically sensitive to the right nouns. Gerhardt is stymied by an apparent cultural inertia that he attributes to the influence of Dante ("Dante will not let us live / always the fields to be harvested / always the same sky above the bent-over backs / earthburdened") and Olson seems to feel that if he could only lead Gerhardt "back far enough" and under his "own steam" (*D*, 40, 41), then his "present" ("a rod of mountain ash" [*D*, 40]) will be worthwhile. Gerhardt's problem, however, is "forgetting" (*D*, 39). He should not, Olson feels, worry about Dante or the smashed crockery of European traditions:

> There are no broken stones, no statues, no images,
>   phrases,

> composition
> otherwise than
> what Creeley and I also have,
> and without reference to
> what reigned in the house
> and is now well dismissed
>
> (D, 41)

Gerhardt might just as well "come here" (to Campeche, where Olson wrote his poem),

> where we will welcome you
> with nothing but what is, with
> no useful allusions, with no birds
> but those we stone, nothing to eat
> but ourselves, no end and no beginning, I assure you,
>   yet
> not at all primitive, living as we do in a space we do
>   not need to contrive
>
> And with our predecessors who, though they are not
>   our nouns,
>   the verbs
> are like!
>
> (D, 42)

The Mayan culture to which Olson refers is the proper gate to the center of the primordial that Gerhardt seeks. Mexico, Olson urges, is as close to a return to Sumer and a truly human universe as one can expect. If Gerhardt can "forget" the barren nominalization he practices in Europe's ruins and effect a proper return to space through Mayan verbs he will then appreciate the "present" (pun intended) Olson feels he has given him.

"Anecdotes of the Late War" is a conspiracy of Herodotus, Carl Sauer, Brooks Adams, and timorous editing. Olson's warning to Cid Corman about the dangers of typographical errors, that "if errors creep in, palpable errors, then the whole careful structure comes down" (LO, 40) seems relevant to this poem, for obvious "palpable errors" have "crept" in and, worse, have been perpetuated by apparently cautious editors both in *The Distances* and *Archaeologist of Morning*. The following items threaten the "whole careful structure" of this poem:

West Point is wasn't . . . [it]
(*D*, 57)

the elevator / goink down . . .
(*D*, 57)

They were—for the first time—enough of them. [There were]
(*D*, 59)

Olson's deliberate "illiteracy" almost obviates complaints such as these, for in most cases a partisan apologist could easily construct a protective rationale for even the most blatant typographical or grammatical offense. Instances like these breed suspicion that perhaps more than a few projective flights of genius might have really been mere typographical blunders. The methodology of this poem is idiosyncratically difficult as it is without interpretive red herrings such as these.

The poem employs the methodology of *'istorin*, Sauer's morphology, and Olson's own iconoclasm to restore a proper stance towards the American Civil War. The opening line sets an atmosphere for debate or at least controversial dogmatics:

the lethargic vs violence as alternatives of each other
for los americanos

The model for lethargy is Ulysses S. Grant, whose career, as it penetrated like a drill through "vice" and "virtue," only displayed Grant's existence—his being—when it happened to strike rock:

he struck, going down, either
morass or

rock—and when it was rock, he was
(*D*, 55)

The poem relentlessly presses the point that Grant was a
dispersed individual whose lethargy made him passively
vulnerable to the "vice" of Galena as well as the "virtue" of
Vicksburg.

John Wilkes Booth is a tentative model for violence and
thus a proper "face off" for Grant. Olson's language reveals his admiration of Booth as a "type": "the face of, blow
/ the earth" (*D*, 55). It recalls Olson's account of "typos" to
Elaine Feinstein: "The 'blow' hits here" (*HU*, 97) and his
explanation of that term elsewhere in an unpublished
essay:

> . . . a type is a blow which characterizes a thing at base
> and as such measures, almost, one might say the sub-
> stantive itself.[15]

Booth, assassin though he was, had the "will to cohere." He
possessed an integrity that focused his energies for use.
Another much like him, whom the poem exploits as
model, is Nathan Bedford Forrest, whose reputation as a
slavetrader and "first Grand Wizard of the Ku Klux Klan"
(*D*, 58) has tarnished his place in history. Not Olson's history, however. Like Booth, Forrest earned Olson's admiration because he was a man "locked in the act of himself . . . very exact and busy . . . an extraordinary executive
/ of men horses and goods" who "applied first principles in
war" (*D*, 58). Despite the history books, it was Forrest, not
Grant, who displayed "*typos*," who "could already avoid the
temptation of the Filibuster," and the other lures of
pejorocracy. The Civil War, in Olson's opinion, was the
"basement" (*D*, 57) of all wars, a fact known only by the
soldiers who actually fought in it ("butternut / and his fel-
low on the other side"). Grant and his kind were not engaged in war but in "real estate" (*D*, 58), going after "what
Jay Gould got," while "Joe Blow got swap / in the side of
the head" (*D*, 57).

The theme of the poem is not particularly novel or arresting. Even though one can see in it the imprint of Sauer's morphological approach to history (not "the energy, customs or beliefs of man but . . . man's record upon the landscape"[16]) and particularization of "evidence" according to Herodotus's definition of history as "finding out for oneself," the poem rehearses the tired old truism that wars are conflicts of political and economic interests rather than men:

> Butternut
> and Yankee Doodle,
> weren't as different as North and South, farmer and
> Factory etc.
> [There] were—for the first time—enough of them.
>
> (*D*, 59)

The energy the poem does project kinetically seems bought at the expense of a split between form and content—that is, the gnomic wonder engineered by violated syntax and odd placements disastrously reveals not the powerful depth of the content it works but its poverty. The unhappy result is the appearance of careless, vituperative opinion begging indulgence because it is "poetry."

There are occasions, not confined to his later work, when Olson permits self-indulgence to compromise the rigor of his conviction that "art is the only morality" (*LO*, 106). The methodology of the open form makes this all but inevitable. The indulgence that Olson allows himself, however, is rarely extended to others, even those to whom he ought to acknowledge his greatest debts. Marjorie Perloff, for example, takes Olson to task for his arrogantly ungrateful remarks about Pound and Williams (his "Inferior predecessors"[17]), and the poem "I, Mencius, Pupil of the Master . . ." serves as an illustration of this tendency. It is a blatant act of diatribe, of the order of the earlier "Letter for Melville: written to be read AWAY FROM the Melville Society's 'One Hundredth Birthday Party' for MOBY-DICK at Williams College . . .," which is best defended as a measure of Olson's dedication to principle rather than politesse.

Apparently upset by Pound's experimental translation of the Odes of Confucius in a deliberately archaic form of regular meter, rhyme, and fixed stanzas, Olson convinced himself that Pound had become a turncoat to his own poetics. Assuming the persona of Mencius, the Chinese philosopher and student of Confucius, Olson proceeds to scold his mentor:

> the dross of verse. Rhyme!
> when iron (steel)
> has expelled Confucius
> from China Pittsburgh!
> beware: the Master
> betrays his vertu.
> To clank like you do
> he brings coolie verse
> to teach you equity,
> who laid down such rails!
> (D, 61)

The poem progresses from scolding to direct insult:

> Who doesn't know a whorehouse
> from a palace . . .
>
> that the great 'ear
> can no longer 'hear

and proceeds dutifully to earn Perloff's censure that it

> is no more than a superficially clever poem. For one thing, Olson's own Rule #3—"ONE PERCEPTION MUST IMMEDIATELY AND DIRECTLY LEAD TO A FURTHER PERCEPTION"—is not observed in this poem, which basically restates the same theme over and over again.[18]

The alleged reiterated theme is the poetics of the earlier Pound, particularly the theme affirmed in Fenollosa's essay:

Noise! that Confucius himself
should try to alter it, he
who taught us all
that no line must sleep,
that as the line goes so goes
the Nation! . . .

that what the eye sees,
that in the East the sun untangles itself
from among branches,
should be made to sound as though there were still
          roads
on which men hustled
to get to paradise, to get to
Bremerton
shipyards!

                                        (*D*, 62)

Pound, Olson charges, violated the law of the line as trans-
fer of force, and he compounded that sin by prostituting
the frozen act of the ideograph (image) to allegory. He in-
vited the "clank" back into his song.

Part III, accordingly, is a rededication to projectivist in-
dependence:

It is too late
to try to teach us
                    we are the process
                      and our feet
                              We do not march
We still look
            And see
                what we see
                        We do not see
                        ballads
      other than our own
                                    (*D*, 63)

"A Newly Discovered 'Homeric' Hymn" chants the
paradoxical admonition "Hail and beware the dead who
will talk life . . ." (*D*, 72) and seems to suggest that these
"dead" possess a valuable wisdom, but a wisdom gained

through inadmissible means: "They come into life / by a different gate . . . from a place which is not easily known." Moreover, they "carry what the living cannot do without." The riddling continues. We learn that these "dead" "are drunk from pot," that they "have the seeds in their mouth," that they "deceive," and that they do not "suffer" but "need, because they have drunk of the pot." They deserve to be hailed, presumably, because "they teach you drunkenness," but you should be wary because "You have your own place to drink."

Superficially, at least, the poem seems to be exploring the propriety of using drugs as a means to achieving the apparently salutary experience of "drunkenness." The conclusion seems to be that they are inappropriate:

> You are not to
> drink. But you must hear, and see. You must beware.
> Hail them, and fall off. Fall off! The drink is not
> yours . . .
>
> (D, 73)

In 1963, seven years after the publication of this poem, Olson taped a discussion at the home of the William Gratwicks in Pavilion, New York, which reveals attitudes relevant to this poem.[19] He attacks the word *hallucinogen* as a "false" characterization of what the particular drugs it refers to actually do. He feels that the so-called hallucinogens simply raise the level of the senses to "what can be nothing more than a normal, real, true character." These drugs "put you on your own autonomic nervous system—as against the motor," he asserts, and goes on to describe this state as one "without the interference of the will." In other words, Olson seems to feel that "hallucinogens" are one means to achieve "negative capability," but when he is asked if it is possible to achieve this state "without the aid of any of these agents," he makes this interesting reply:

> I do. Certainly I do. Otherwise I'd be using that stuff I've got in Gloucester. . . . But it's not easy to achieve.

And certainly the human race has been so bereft of its
autonomic system for so long that you can practically
talk that we're green

The poem's earlier view toward drugs seems more conservatively opposed to artificial means of activating the
autonomic system, but Olson's consistent wariness of drugs
("I've only been under any of these drugs twice in my
life . . .") seems to re-affirm that position. The real theme
of the poem, as opposed to the drug medium used to present it, seems once again to be the sense of loss man has
allowed himself to experience because he has permitted
his "irritable reaching after fact and reason" to shut off the
necessary "drunkenness" he also requires. The appeal to
the demonic in our nature is certainly made in the poem,
but the hallucinogenic route to the demonic is held suspect
because it is artificial and addictive: "they need, because
they have drunk of the pot."
Beneath the appeal to "drunkenness" and the caveat
against drugs resides the Jungian notion that the inner
movement of human life is seeking to redress an imbalance. Heraclitus, Jung notes, called this inner movement
enantiodromia (a term Olson adopts as the title of the final
chapter in *The Special View of History*), "a running con-
trarywise, by which he meant that sooner or later everything runs to its opposite."[20] Olson's "'Homeric' Hymn"
acknowledges the fatal allure of each of these opposites by
recommending that the redressing of imbalance be initiated with caution. The rejuvenation of the "dead" in us,
our demonic dark side quickened through drunkenness,
must be accomplished with care:

> Beware the dead. And hail them. They teach you
> drunkenness.
> You have your own place to drink. Hail and beware
>   them, when
>   they come.

> (*D*, 73)

They *do* come in *The Distances* in "The Lordly and Isolate
Satyrs." A motorcycle gang occasions a demonstration of

Jung's conviction that "to confront a person with his shadow is to show him his low light. . . . Anyone who perceives his shadow and his light simultaneously sees himself from two sides and thus gets in the middle. He knows that the world consists of darkness and light. I can master the polarity only by freeing myself from them by contemplating both, and so reaching a middle position. Only than am I no longer at the mercy of the opposites."[21]

Olson's satyrs strike him as Androgynes... Great Halves" (D, 82). They are, just as the "drunken dead" in "A Newly Discovered 'Homeric' Hymn," complementary shadows and we are advised to "hail them, and watch out" (D, 83), for we are as yet unfamiliar with "this left side" of our human existence. These unknown "leftists" on motorcycles are "our counterparts, the unknown ones," but they "are not gods. . . . They are doubles. They are only Source" (D, 84). Thus, Olson identifies his lordly and isolate satyrs as demonic nourishment, dionysian "drunkenness," and "Fathers behind the father" (D, 82). The momentary fusion of their primordial darkness with our conscious light miraculously reveals "the beach we had not known was there" (D, 83). The balance of dark and light, to translate the phenomenon into Olson's terms, makes possible "projective size" (HU, 60):

> The Visitors—Resters—who, by being there,
> made manifest what we had now known—that the
>   beach fronted wholly
> to the sea—have only done that, completed the
>   beach
>
> (D, 84)

George Oppen cited this poem as the one in *The Distances* that most successfully escapes the influence of Pound, "in which the voice and eye are his [Olson's] alone."[22] Thom Gunn's more hostile view of the poem doesn't quarrel with that point, but wonders whether Olson's "voice and eye" have much poetic skill. He feels that Olson "has little interest in the sensible world except as a handle on which to hang bits of poetry" and he illustrates the remark with the opening of "The Lordly and Isolate Satyrs":

> Wow, did you ever see even in a museum
> such a collection of boddisatvahs, the way
> they came to their stop, each of them
> as though it was a rudder
> the way they have to sit above it
> and come to a stop on it, the monumental solidity
> of themselves, the Easter Island
> they make of the beach, the Red-headed Men.

Gunn's complaint is that "in the whole poem there is little description of them, evocation of them, as they are: they continually are described in terms of what they are not. The things they are not (Androgynes, etc.) are evoked, it seems, purely at random: the poem consists merely of a gigantic list of associations accumulated at whim."[23]

Gunn's criticism, while pictorially trenchant, appears to assume that Olson's subject is the motorcyclists *as motorcyclists*. In fact, Olson is only interested in them as satyrs, as his title (to be fair) clearly indicates. Thus, Olson is justified in describing his motorcyclists as "they are not" because it is precisely the subtle demonic "notness" about them that he wishes to evoke.

Following as it does "A Newly Discovered 'Homeric' Hymn," "As the Dead Prey upon Us" cannot help but bear some of the lingering freight from its predecessor's closing lines: "Beware the dead. And hail them" (*D*, 73). Indeed, an ambivalent "hail" and "beware" attitude toward the dead obscures the meaning of the opening stanza of this long dream meditation:

> As the dead prey upon us,
> they are the dead in ourselves,
> awake, my sleeping ones, I cry out to you,
> disentangle the nets of being!

On the one hand the dead "prey upon us" like some internal malignancy and yet it appears as if they are also being evoked for a salutary purpose: to "disentangle the nets of being." Is this a petition directed to the demonic shadow of our being (the dead) to enrich us with drunkenness so that we might escape the cold hell of our encumbered lives?

Apparently not. The "dead souls" that actually respond to the summons in stanza three are not demonic nourishers but victims themselves of "the tawdriness of their life in hell." They are unlikely candidates for the challenge of "disentangling the nets of being," because as they roam "from one to another / as bored back in life as they are in hell, poor and doomed / to mere equipments," they transform the whole living room into a hellish museum of contemporary entanglements:

> And the whole room was suddenly posters and pre-
> sentations of brake linings and other automotive acces-
> sories, cardboard displays. . . .

This hell that they evoke is sufficiently vivid to impress us with its *un*reality. The "projector," the "posters," the "cardboard displays," the "mere equipments" all suggest the representations of Plato's parable of the cave. The *living*room of the poem consists of bogus encumbrances that intervene between us and the familiarly real. Even the enigmatic humanizing of the "blue deer" by the "Indian woman and I" (*D*, 75) only serves to underscore the *in*humanity of the livingroom poseurs. It is "cold hell" all over again.

Some specificity is lent to the "nets" that entangle lives by the allusion to the "five hindrances" of Buddhism (*D*, 75): "1) sensuality or greed 2) ill-will 3) sloth or torpor 4) worry and flurry and 5) doubt."[24] These hindrances enmesh men, angels, and demons in "immense nets / which spread out across the plane of being" (*D*, 75) and restrain them from "Purity." Oddly, the perfection, that "Purity," is in fact "hidden" within the five hindrances and is described as "an instant of being." In this description resides the secret of escape.

"Paradise," the poem tells us, is not only "happiness" but it is also "the instant" (*D*, 77). The eternal hell of the "dead souls" consists in the fact that they are condemned forever to "coming back, returning / to the instants which were not lived" (*D*, 78). The saving truth that the speaker in the poem reveals is:

> I am myself netted in my own being
> (*D*, 78)

This means that the knots of the net are not impediments that constrain, but are actually "flames" (*D*, 80), or better, walls "ready to be shot open by you" (*D*, 81). The knots are instants of "now"—pure spontaneity. That which detracts one's care and attention from the instant is "cheapness," the "crankcase of an ugly automobile," "the sodden weights of goods, / equipment, entertainment, the foods the Indian woman, / the filthy blue deer, the 4 by 3 foot 'Viewbook,' / the heaviness of the old house, the stuffed inner room" (*D*, 78)—in a word, hell.

In terms of practical counsel, the poem offers a simple solution to the problem of dealing with knots as spontaneous opportunities rather than eternal barriers:

> the nets of being
> are only eternal if you sleep as your hands
> ought to be busy. Method, method
>
> I call on you to come
> to the aid of all men
> (*D*, 81)

Gerald Van de Wiele was a young art student at Black Mountain College and the "Variations" that Olson dedicates to him seem like responses to some kind of poetic challenge. It is as if Olson wished to demonstrate his virtuosity to skeptics by deliberately aping the poetic styles of others. Section I is clearly a prosodic retort to William Carlos Williams, which a cursory comparison to "Portrait of a Lady" will instantly reveal. Similarly, the pattern of the variations themselves echoes Wallace Stevens's "Sea Surface Full of Clouds." Hints of Yeats and Pound might also be detected, but predictably, even in conscious imitation, Olson's "blind obedience" to "personage" never quite permits him to sustain the integrity of each variation. Each section inevitably closes with an unmistakable Olson signature.

Olson takes his theme directly from Rimbaud's *"O saisons, o Chateaux"* from *Une Saison en Enfer*. The lines that he particularly favors with adaptive appreciation are these:

> *Ce charme a pris âme et corps*
> *Et disperse les efforts.*
> > *O saisons, o chateaux!*

The charm of the seasons that seizes the mind and the body and disperses their efforts is treated in these three varied modes by Olson:

1)   the seasons
      seize
      the soul and the body, and make mock
      of any dispersed effort. The hour of death
      is the only trespass . . .

                                      (*D*, 87)

2)   do you know the charge,
      that you shall have no envy, that your life
      has its orders, that the seasons
      seize you too, that no body and soul are one
      if they are not wrought
      in this retort? that otherwise efforts
      are efforts? And that the hour of your flight
      will be the hour of your death? . . .

                                      (*D*, 88)

3)   Envy
      drags herself off. The fault of the body and
            soul
      —that they are not one—
      the matitudinal cock clangs

and singleness: we salute you
season of no bungling
(D, 89)

Olson typically wrenches an apparent pastoral mood into
an epistemological stance. The power of the season brings
body and soul into healthy unity and thus effectuates that
Sumerian "will to cohere," which "mocks" effete dispersion. Moreover, the second variation emphasizes Olson's
commitment to an obedience ("your life has its orders").
Knowledge that we are properly obedient creatures beholden to the dictates of the "life within us" removes our
"envy" of Spring, that is, an envy that is a symptom of the
"lyrical interference of the individual as ego" (HU, 59). In
short, these "Variations" diagnose the human malady once
again as a split between mind and body—"that they are not
one" (D, 89)—and prescribes the cure: "singleness"—the
reintegration with "that with which we are most familiar."

Charles Olson was fond of alluding to Carl Jung's notion
that

> the self is not only the centre but also the whole circum-
> ference which enhances both the conscious and the un-
> conscious; it is the center of this totality, just as the ego is
> the centre of the conscious mind.[25]

Olson's persona, Maximus, as he functions both in *The
Maximus Poems* and here in "The Librarian," is the embodiment of the kind of circumferential self that Jung describes and that Jung himself labeled "homo maximus."
Maximus moves freely over inward and outward land-
scapes, ignoring the boundaries that usually divide them.
In doing so, he illuminates a composite truth that includes
both dark and light sides of human experience. As trope,
Maximus enjoys liberties normally available only to dream.

In "The Librarian" Maximus is a "duplicate" (D, 90). His
"off-shore" entity is "removed" from his "shore one." Even
his act of viewing Gloucester's landscape is itself a duplica-
tion: "(the landscape!) again." Butterick writes that "Olson
spoke of Gloucester as having 'interested me because it sits

on the Atlantic, and therefore I can say I come from the east,' and that 'Maximus himself [Maximus of Tyre] . . . is a person who speaks from further east than Gloucester to the city.'"[26] In one sense this accounts for the duplications, but in another Jungian sense it is tempting to see the two Maximi as separate functions of the same entity—one, for example, the center and the other, the circumference of the self.

Charles Boer writes,

> I should comment here, Charles, on how sensitive you were to landscapes—especially Gloucester landscapes. You would often pause for long periods outdoors to stare at things—a sunset, a tree, the angle of a stone wall, the location of an old house, and of course the sea, the omnipresent Gloucester sea. . . . And you described what you saw with a painter's precision rather than a poet's license.[27]

But there is little of the "painter's precision" in "The Librarian." The terrain of truth that Maximus/Olson seeks in this poem is not of such conscious visual substance. Here Maximus moves on "the territory with combinations / (new mixtures) of old and known personages" (D, 90). His vehicle of entry into the city is people who, for one reason or another, have deeply touched him and, presumably, still strike chords in his unconscious. Maximus seeks out these "personages" not willfully but as if in obedience to the logic of dreams.

The fluidity of dream permits the conscious object of Maximus's quest, his father, to reform into "the young musician" who, enigmatically, has "(been before me)" (D, 90). The musician is a dark, offending entity who has "presented . . . insinuations" and, worse, "had been in my parents' bedroom where I / found him intimate with my former wife." Maximus himself is aware that he is indiscriminately mixing central and circumferential matters. He admits that he had known the young musician and his girl "for years. / But never in Gloucester. I had moved them in, to my country" (D, 90). The country is clearly a landscape bounded by the circumference of Maximus's total awareness, and the young musician impresses his dark identity indelibly into Gloucester's reality by becoming the librarian. The poem depicts the librarian as a stain, an encroachment, an invasion by an alien, even a betrayer. Maximus "dogs" his steps, and the two, with "Motions / of ghosts," pass into the "Black space" of the fish house.

Images of alienation and separation precipitate. The librarian, we learn, had set up a poetry reading from which Maximus was excluded ("It was not for me. I was outside"). In a coal house "a gang / was beating someone to death, . . . and the cops / tailed me along the Fort Beach toward the Tavern" (*D*, 91). In the midst of all these dark image-events is the potentially redeeming knowledge "that my daughter / was there. . . . That she was there (in the Promised Land—the Cut)" (*D*, 91). But the image of the daughter at the Cut (the Blynman Canal in Gloucester where each year on a Sunday in August relatives and friends of the fishermen gather to throw bouquets of flowers on the outgoing tide) affords only enough light to deepen the shadows cast by the other images of the poem. Maximus's quest for "materials" (*D*, 90) has ended in his being "caught in Gloucester" (*D*, 92), but it is a Gloucester with which he is no longer familiar:

> Where
> is Bristow? when does 1-A
> get me home? . . .
> (What's buried
> behind Lufkin's
> Diner? Who is
> Frank Moore?

The dream images of "The Librarian" are deeply and darkly personal, even more so than even the most attentive reader can be aware. Boer, for instance, after asking Olson what was buried behind Lufkin's Diner, reports his reply:

> You laughed. "Who do you think is buried there?" you asked.

> I told you I had no idea.
> "Lufkin, you dope!"
> And yet, as I was to learn much later, it is not
> Lufkin at all who is buried behind Lufkin's Diner.
> In fact nobody is. You had had a dream in which
> two children were murdured and buried there. In
> the dream, you saw them as "lovekin." The joke
> was on me. Twice.[28]

"The Librarian," then, might finally be understood as a treatment of the murder of love and kinship in the circumferential landscape of Maximus's Gloucester, that is, Maximus's total conscious and unconscious self. Distances have intervened between father and son, father and daughter, husband and wife, a man and his art, Maximus and his city.The integrity of what is familiar has been severed. The Cut, with all its funereal implications of loss, is finally the deepest and saddest cut of all.

The Cut appears again in the next poem, "Moonset, Gloucester, December 1, 1957, 1:58 A M," which, if it were not for the anomalous dates, might seem a bitter elegy for the death of his mother. Olson's mother, Mary, actually died on Christmas day, 1950, and the other specific date cited in the poem, "After 47 years this month / a Monday at 9 A M" (D, 93) obviously refers to Olson's own birth. The poem seems to punctuate some turning point in Olson's life:

> you set I rise I hope
> a free thing . . .

as if the death of Mary was a significant divestiture of inhibiting authority. In *Maximus IV, V, VI* Olson writes, ". . . a mother is a hard thing to get away from . . ." (M, 37) and some of that rueful acknowledgment informs the climactic passage of "Moonset":

> Rise
> Mother from off me
> God damn you God damn me my

misunderstanding of you

I can die now I just begin to live.

What personal energies charged this poem one can only speculate on. At the date he wrote it he had just finished the unpleasant duty of selling off the Black Mountain property and had returned to Gloucester to begin his second run of the *Maximus* sequence (*Maximus IV, V, VI*). More than likely he felt strongly that his life was taking a new direction and perhaps required some ritualistic re-dedication that the poem supplied. Certainly, the coincidence of his mother's name with the Virgin lends some credence to Robert Bertholf's speculation that the moon stands for the "female force" (anima) that is associated with a "Mary complex," the removal of which "brings a freedom from the obligations of the past."[29] At any rate, the short poem is movingly occasional even though that occasion remains obscure.

The final poem in *The Distances*, from which the volume takes its name, is about the distances that, in one way or another, concern all the poems in the collection—distances that are evident when men cease in their lives and their art to be "equal to the real itself" (*HU*, 117). "The Distances" catalogues a number of separations: "Old Zeus—young Augustus," Pygmalion and his statue, a German inventor and his paramour (a dead Cuban corpse). The ending offers a final remedy for all distances through Aphrodite and her life-giving gesture to Pygmalion's stone:

O love who places all where each is, as they are, for
                every moment,
    yield
        to this man
                        that the impossible distance
    be healed,
                    that young Augustus
                    and old Zeus
    be enclosed

"I awake you,
stone. Love this man."
(D, 95–96)

Aphrodite's words are not only the rite that brings
Galatea to life for her artist lover but they articulate as well
the rite that all artists hope to perform: waking beauty out
of stone. Olson's enduring commitment to the living art of
Mayan glyphs makes such stony awakenings even more
poetically significant, but in the end it is still love that heals
"the impossible distance" (D, 95), that separates the divine
and the human (Zeus and Augustus), and that permits
their incorporation into one integral and very "human
universe" in which it is not implausible at all for objets d'art
to bear the charge: "Love this man."

NOTES

1. "The E at Delphi," *Plutarch's Moralia*, trans. Frank Cole Babbit,
   Loeb Classical Library (Cambridge, Mass.: Harvard University
   Press, 1936), 5:391e.
2. Ezra Pound, "How to Read," *Literary Essays of Ezra Pound* (New
   York: New Directions, 1968), p. 37.
3. Robert Creeley, "Some Notes on Olson's *Maximus*," in *Yugen 8* (New
   York: Totem Press, [1962]), p. 52.
4. Unpubl. essay entitled "Pun as True Meaning as Well as of Rhyme"
   (*CtU*).
5. See Ann Charters, *Olson/Melville: A Study in Affinity* (Berkeley,
   Calif.: Oyez, 1968), p. 86.
6. Olson's source for the Thomas Granger incident is *Bradford's History "Of Plimouth Plantation"* (Boston: Wright and Patter Printing
   Company, 1891), pp. 456–60, 468, 471, 474–75.
7. See the illustration that Robert Bertholf provides in "Righting the
   Balance: Olson's *The Distances*," *Boundary 2* 2 (Fall 1973/Winter
   1974): 249n1.
8. Olson, "Notes for the Proposition: Man Is Prospective," *Boundary 2*
   2 (Fall 1973/Winter 1974): 2.
9. Charles Olson, *Stocking Cap* (San Francisco: Four Seasons Foundation, 1966).
10. Olson, "Notes for the Proposition: Man Is Prospective," p. 2.
11. Ibid., p. 3.
12. Ibid., p. 4.

13. Richard G. Ingber, "Number, Image, Sortilege: A Short Analysis of 'The Moon Is the Number 18,'" *Boundary 2* 2 (Fall 1973/Winter 1974): 270.

14. Rainer Maria Gerhardt, "Letter for Greeley and Olson," *Origin* 4 (Winter 1952): 187–93; Olson, *The Distances*, pp. 241–48.

15. Olson, "There are four measurements . . ." (*CtU*)

16. Carl Ortwin Sauer, *Land and Life*, ed. John Leighly (Berkeley, Calif.: University of California Press, 1967), p. 342.

17. "Charles Olson and the 'Inferior Predecessors': 'Projective Verse' Revisited," *ELH* 40 (Summer 1973): 285–306.

18. Ibid., p. 299.

19. Charles Olson, "Under the Mushroom: The Gratwick Highlands Tape," *Olson* 3 (Spring 1975): 3–57.

20. Carl Jung, *The Collected Works*, Bollingen Series 20, 2d ed. (Princeton, N.J.: Princeton University Press, 1957), 7:71.

21. Ibid., 10:463–64.

22. George Oppen, review of *Maximus from Dogtown, Poetry* 100 (August 1962): 332.

23. Thom Gunn, "New Books in Review," *Yale Review* 50 (Summer 1961): 595.

24. See Robert Bertholf, "Righting the Balance," p. 244.

25. Jung, *Collected Works*, 12:41. See also Olson's allusions to "the center and the circumference" (*SVH*, 36, 37, 45).

26. George Butterick, "A Guide to the Maximus Poems of Charles Olson," Ph.D. diss., State University of New York at Buffalo, 1970, p. 2.

27. Charles Boer, *Charles Olson in Connecticut* (Chicago: Swallow Press, 1975), p. 57.

28. Ibid., p. 150.

29. Bertholf, "Righting the Balance," pp. 247–48.

5

Archaeologist of Morning

Nature, like god,
is not so interesting. Man
is interesting
—"The Post Virginal"

In 1973 a collection of every poem Charles Olson authorized for publication (including the poems of *The Distances* but excluding the *Maximus* sequence) was published under the title *Archaeologist of Morning*. This intriguing sobriquet originates in an essay Olson once wrote called "The Present Is Prologue" in which he confesses,

> ...I find it awkward to call myself a poet or a writer. If there are no walls there are no names. This is the morning after the dispersion, and the work of the morning is methodology: how to use oneself, and on what. That is my profession. I am an archaeologist of morning. (*AP*, 40)

Olson always felt the constraint of job descriptions. Once, when was asked what he taught at Black Mountain, he quipped, "I teach posture,"[1] and toward the end of his career he tended to favor "mythologist" as the best description of his métier. But all of these titles—professor of posture, mythologist, archaeologist of morning—are more than vocations; they establish a "stance towards reality," a prescription of "how to use oneself, and on what," a methodology for living. They also represent a backward look. They recommend an epistemology anterior to our present one of dispersion, a leap-frogging into the Sumerian past over the smothering blanket of Hellenism in between.[2]

In spite of a misleading Hellenic veneer covering some,

all of the poems in *Archaeologist of Morning* do, in one way or another, bear arms against dispersion and do grope toward that Sumerian ideal: "the WILL TO COHERE" (*HU*, 21). Their methodology, however, at least in a narrow poetic sense, is not always as consistently doctrinaire as one might expect. Because of its inclusiveness, the collection is not as overtly "composed" as *The Distances* and provides a more comprehensive appreciation of Olson's range.

For example, with a poet committed to testing how far he can "stretch the very conventions on which communication by language rests" (*HU*, 56), it is reassuring to see that, if he chooses, he does possess the formal ability to "do it straight." The opening poem of *Archaeologist of Morning*, "Lower Field—Enniscorthy," shows Olson at his straightest. Here the pressure of projective dogma is relatively absent. The poem is a simple pastoral. Without embarrassment it luxuriates in description of the Virginia landscape and unabashedly traffics in comparisons, rhymes, similes, and even allegory. Far from kinetic act, the poem is in fact a still-life energized by trope.

> The sheep like soldiers
> black leggings black face
> lie boulders
> in the pine's shade
> at the field's sharp edge:
> ambush and bivouac
>
> A convocation of crows overhead
> mucks
> in their own mud and squawk
> makes of the sky
> a sty
>
> A bee is deceived
> takes the rot of a stump
> for honeycomb
>
> Two black snakes cross
> in a flat spiral
> the undisciplined path

Report: over all
the sun.[3]

While one might detect inchoate shadows of the projective here and there, this is unquestionably a "literary"
poem. "Devices" saturate its fabric. The "metaphysical"
comparison of sheep and soldier effectively charges the
static scene with metaphorical tension prompted by "am-
bush and bivouac." The forceful "muck," accompanied by
"mud," "sty," and "squawk," synaesthetically provides an
arresting environment for the "convocation' of crows. The
"deceived bee"—a blatant pathetic fallacy—along with the
suggestion of Eden achieved by the spiraling snakes, also
overtly pumps "meaning" into the poem and thus sets up
the final provocative enigma of the last two lines, which,
themselves, pick up the military metaphor of the first
stanza with an official "morning report." The poem is an
achievement that comforts explicators.

"A Lion Upon the Floor" is another matter. While it may
seem to have superficial similarities to Wallace Stevens's
"Poetry Is a Destructive Force," and while it may yield effective energy to those unfamiliar with the "stance," it
nevertheless hews closely to the Olson posture and the
Olson methodology. It employs one of Olson's apparently
favorite devices, serial opposition, in which the modified
nursery rhyme ("Sing a Song of Six Pence") is juxtaposed
and interspersed with qualifying stanzas heavy with the
usual Olson biases:

> Begin a song
> Power and the abstract
> distract a man
> from his own gain
> Begin a song of six cents

The poem practices what it preaches. The reader is "dis-
tracted" as he alternately shifts from song to abstraction.
"Power" (probably Keats's "Man of power") and "the

abstract" (Keats's "irritable reaching after fact and reason") are distractions that curtail man's natural gain (size).
It is the "song" that deserves his care and attention, but
even the song reveals its peculiar didacticism: "Begin a
song of six cents." "Pence" to "cents" is not merely the
Americanization of English currency but an appeal
(through pun) that we seek our gain through a sixth sense,
probably the bodily sense that Olson describes in *Proprioception* (*AP*, 17–19) and what Whitehead calls "causal efficacy"[4]—the sense, ultimately, of being "a thing among
things" without "lyrical interference of the ego" (*HU*, 59),
in a word, "objectism."

  Power and the abstract also

> foul his eye
> deprive his hand upon a nape and hips
> of kiss beak claw

They are responsible not merely for visual pollution but
tactile disability as well. They keep us from the direct, immediate experience of the physicality of existence. The
lion is on the floor. He has been literally "floored" by
power and the abstract, and the poem is an attempt to
rouse him. At this point the serially opposed lines become
appositives:

>   Sing a song
> Let the salt in
> begin
> cut the heart open
> the blood will run with the sun

To sing a song is to let salt in, to cut the heart open and let
the blood run free. Olson's allusion is to the intense physicality of the Aztec sacrifices, which cut out the hearts of
living victims. His view of such rites is not ethical but ap-
provingly aesthetic in the sense that such ceremonies are
"a means of expression the equal of . . . nature's intricacy"

(*HU*, 8). Thus, the re-establishment of a proper stance to nature accordingly accomplishes a re-naturalization of man:

> the blood will run with the sun
> the wind will put the belly back
> and the rain the roar below

Man will once again be obedient to natural forces and all that he awaits is for the lion to spring.

"Troilus" is an attempt to define love, but not in the sentimental terms of Cressida's betrayal of her Trojan lover, as its title suggests. Certainly Troilus serves as a model for the loss of love, which is the poem's concern, but the opening line clearly informs us that Olson means the present day: "Love is not present now, / has flown." We are, in a sense, all Troiluses, the poem assumes, all having been deserted by our beloved (in this case Nature), whom we turned into "whore." Love is not present now because that to which it is the key, Nature, has been prostituted. Actually, the poem surrenders much of its confusion when it is read against Olson's passage in "The Human Universe," which details the very process by which man turned Nature into a whore: The notions of man

> as the center of phenomenon [*sic*] by fiat or of god as the center and man as god's chief reflection ... both set aside nature as an unadmitted or suppressed third party, ... The result, we have been the witness of: discovering this discarded thing nature, science has run away with everything. Tapping her power, fingering her like a child, giving her again her place, but without somehow, remembering what truth there was in man's centering the use of anything, god, devil, or holy ghost, in himself, science has upset all balance and blown value, man's peculiar responsibility, to the winds. (*HU*, 8–9)

Science, in other words, has picked up the girl we cast aside, and we no longer accord her the value that only we

can bestow. Like Troilus we have disvalued our Cressida.
As a result, the path of love is strewn with

                    papers, dust
        cloth (strips which give no clue
        dropped without care
        picked up, lamely, at a dare)

Genuine love will take us back to "that feature nature wore
/ before man turned her, woman, whore," for

        The path, love is the path
                            And in the forest calls,
                                    calls!
        We shall answer, find.
                            But if love now is lust
        or mere drift back
        better we know, and say
        we do not know the way

        The way, love is
        the way!

With its impressive ending and its careful utilization of
rhyme, "Troilus" is more deliberately stylized than the
poems that come after 1950; stylized, that is, nonprojec-
tively. Even so, it contains abundant previews of coming
attractions, as, for example, the celebration of "breath,"
the suspicion towards the notion of love as an abstract
ideal, man's prostitution of nature, and even the wary
premonition that although "love is the way," unattended,
such ways disappear. *"Der Weg stirbt,"* says Olson in "The
Human Universe" (*HU*, 3). Love, in "Troilus," is the bond
that reassembles "dispersion"; it "alone is key to, form /
that feature nature wore / before man turned her, woman,
whore."

An equally strong confidence in the salutory power of
love informs the curiously hortatory carpe diem theme of
"Only the Red Fox, Only the Crow." Here the dead in-
struct the living on vital priorities:

> You who come after us
> you who can live when we are not
> make much of love

But the carpe diem here is no rationalization for immediate indulgence, as it traditionally is, but it is pressed as a formal obligation:

> You who shall have the earth,
> and one another,
> the government of noon
> do not fail us, dance

The appeal is really ontological, for love is championed as a conqueror of time. It bridges generations and links the living and the dead:

> And when, on summer field
> two horses run for joy
> like figures on a beach
> your mind will find us,
> as we have found,
> within its reach.

The total glorification of even the "envy" in love's "blind glance" and the willing subjugation to "the government of noon" unmistakably assert Olson's enduring conviction that love is a "visible truth" that is apprehended in the "absolute condition of present things" (*HU*, 118). Love is indeed "timeless" but not because it is eternal but because it is *now*.

One can detect in these early poems a subtle formal struggle between traditional and projective drives. As if not quite certain of himself in the "open field," Olson nervously cleaves to comforting traditional landmarks both formal and thematic. "In the Hills South of Capernaum, Port" is a clever dramatic construction that resuscitates Christ as its persona and has him comment on the Mosaic decalogue. It is heavy with puns ("as salt, keep your savour [saviour]"), but even more interestingly it presents its Christian "intensification" of the old commandments with a distinctly Olsonian cast. For example, allegiance to the familiar, the natural, is cited as the principle injunction:

Take the natural for base
assume your nature as a bird his or the grass.

These lines anticipate "The Human Universe":

Man has made himself an ugliness and a bore. It was better to be a bird, as these Maya seem to have been, they kept moving their heads so nervously to stay alive, to keep alerted to what they were surrounded by. (*HU*, 12)

In spite of its saturation with the usual Olson themes, the poem as a whole seems overly derivative, contrived, and ultimately not very conclusive as the ethical "intensification" it pretends to be. The energy with which Olson later will hurl his ethical dogmas suffers serious attrition here, perhaps because it rides so obviously piggy-back on standard gospel injunctions.

"The Story of Olson and Bad Thing" was written in early June, 1950, and first appeared in *Origin* 1 (Spring 1951). Like "The Kingfishers," it rides close to the bone of Olson's major preoccupations, containing, in fact, inchoate notions that soon would find fuller blossoming in "Projective Verse," "The Human Universe," and "The Resistance." It is itself an intimate gathering of the fragrance of violets (an image Olson takes from Bolyai Farkas), which it identifies as "the smell of life"; in particular, one is tempted to add, the smell of Olson's life that it celebrates.

"Bad Thing" is an unparticularized enemy (although most would brutally reduce it, when pressed, to Time) who comes in the night and eats at the heart and the intestines. He is opposed and resisted by man's sheer stubbornness, particularly the stubbornness of "olson males" who smell of violets and "live up to . . . the affections." Olson's own father, for example, died because of a stubbornness that affected not his nerves but his blood vessels, the poem tells us, "where the fragrance is." Just as in "Troilus" and "Only the Red Fox, Only the Crow," the "affections" (love) and the sheer immediate life of violets (spontaneous joy) are trusted to protect us from "Bad Thing," but as Olson ruminates on his own predicament, he concludes that his fate will be different from his father's because of an additional stubbornness brought on by his realization that "my time is quantitative and / must thus, be turned to space." Here, again, Olson voices his confidence in space that promises, "in antithesis to time, secrets of a humanitas eased out of contemporary narrows."[5] Later in the poem he specifically cites "the easing of space" as a primary defense against "Bad Thing."

Precisely how space successfully frustrates the tyranny of time is obscure in the poem and even Olson's prose explanations are not extremely clear. In "Notes for the Proposition: Man is Prospective," for instance, he writes:

> man as object in space as against man as subject of time makes possible a life-death concept which admits man's reflection as force in nature . . . .
> If science will now do the one last thing man has a right to ask of it—teach man how to restore nature's intention with his organism, that he live an animal span of some 130 years, science can go the way of magic and religion.[6]

Space, it seems, promises no immortality but simply the natural fulfillment of man's 130-year life span. Thus, Olson's vow in the poem takes on more coherence:

> I must not break, must, somehow,
> haul myself up eighty years

Why he does not go for the full 130 years is not clear, but there is no mistaking that the "return to space" is tantamount to the same willful rejection of Time's ravages that Love is capable to effect. Space is the "condition of present things," an acceptance of now.

The opening of this poem is charged with unsorted

energies that disclose their integrity only from the vantage of Olson's "stance towards reality." For example, the violets of Bolyai senior (a leitmotif throughout the poem) solicit our obedience, calling up through their "smell of life," the life in us—"that which we are in the hands of." According to Bolyai, men spring up like violets on the hillside in Spring when they are needed and confirm what Whitehead calls the "creative aim" of the universe. Olson, in fact, once specifically cited Whitehead himself as one such hillside violet:

> So it comes out like those violets of Bolyai Senior on all sides when men are needed, that we possess a body of thinking the order of Whitehead's to catch us up where we wouldn't naturally poke our hearts in and to intensify our own thought just where it does poke.[7]

Another is Olson's own father, whose burst blood vessels revealed at his death "where / the fragrance is."

The poem thus speaks of and to an elite who obey the fragrance of their blood by living with the affections and stubbornly defying Time's fraudulent three-score-ten limitation to human life. Part 2 develops the notion further by insisting that what we lack is not intelligence but stamina. "Shortness of life (what Bad / Thing feeds on, knows how to nibble at" is what the creator damned the race with. Presumably men can overcome that damnation simply by following the regimen of a different authority:

> And that which we go by
> in the running, breath, breath, which can, as the flesh
> can, give off
> the odor of, same flowers

Apparently the saving authority of "space" has been particularized in the "breath," but since the "return to space" reduces to a commitment to the restoration of a normal lifespan, then breath, as the fundamental act of the body's proprioceptive functioning, seems reasonably synonymous.

If the "smell of violets" is the appropriate atmosphere

for men, its negative counterpart is "the whole stink" of original sin that, we are reminded, western culture has converted to "the smell of . . . the fast buck." Like Lear, Olson yearns for an "ounce of civet" to sweeten the stench of his imagination and to neutralize the "smell of mortality":

> kill, kill! he cried
> just to get rid of, just
> to avoid
>
> borning, borning, old Bitch Goddess!
> you know
> the answer

> It takes blood, my fellow cits., even to the breaking of vessels!
>   (Vessels!)

"Vessels" introduces the notion of an escape to "the ease" of an alternative culture, one that is "spatial," not temporal. Here Olson seems to anticipate, as he did in "The Kingfishers," his trip to Mexico:

> And he says, It sounds easy, only it ain't, as he dressed himself in doeskin, and went off trading among distant tribes, went looking for a place where people are still natives, and where human business is still the business.

Part 3 uses the violets' smell as a kind of antirationalist touchstone:

> . . .the brains . . . always wants
> what it can't have because they ain't
>
> Answers, I mean,
> which have no smell at all

And more explicit tactics against the ravages of "Bad Thing" are suggested in Part 4, where "time" itself speaks:

"The only trick, the only way to save your thing, or
        whatever, is
obey, obey, until you've squeezed out of, out of me,
        out of me who
is yr onlie true enemie . . ."
The sweetest kind of essence, violets

This ability to squeeze the smell of violets from time is re-
stricted to an elite:

                only those with
the nose for it can smell and
CAN GIVE OFF [the fragrance]

One of the elite—he who quested after the ease "among
distant tribes" in Part 3, in fact—returns in Part 4 and the
poet muses,

                wasn't it curious, that the point at
        which
he emerged should have been already called, by the
        natives, the place
of the heart?

        His quest has been a success. He has learned, among
                other things, how
        properly to dispose of the things he makes:

                        instead of disposing of them in
        so many ways that would occur to you, he merely set
                them out there
        where the rest of the causes of confusion are.

What the quester has learned in "the place of the heart" is
the lesson of "objectism" (*HU*, 59–60): to leave the "difficulties" in his finished work and thus have his art "twin"
rather than mime nature.
    The remainder of the poem builds on this objectist base.
The "return to space" means a restoration of the "familiar"
and thus a liberation from time and discourse, which in-

hibit man from taking his "place alongside the things of nature" (*HU*, 60). In the end, all we have to do is "go / by the nose," follow the "smell of violets" and appreciate "why there is so much blood / all over the place."

When Olson ended his political career in 1945 he was conscious not only of the significance of this vocational change but that he responded once again to that call to obedience emanating from the "life within him." "I wrote 'The K,' the go-away poem shortly after the inauguration of that year,"[8] he explains, suggesting perhaps that the "answer" his poem boldly hurls is no mere personal justification, but a national one as well:

> Take, then, my answer:
> there is a tide in a man
> moves him to his moon and,
> though it drop him back
> he works through ebb to mount
> the run again and swell
> to be tumescent I

Like "The Moon Is the Number 18," this poem takes its inspiration from the tarot pack and in the spirit of the vocational crisis that Olson and the nation apparently share, it sees the tides of man and nation pulled by "lunar" forces beyond conscious human control. That sense of fatalism emerges in the recurring concern with life span ("I shall not see the year 2000 / unless I stem straight from my father's mother, / break the fatal male small span") and is explicit in the lines,

> Is it of such concern when what shall be
> already is within the moonward sea?

Fatal inevitability provides even a rich measure of cultural optimism:

> Full circle: an end to romans, hippocrats and
>   christians.
> There! is a tide in the affairs of men to discern

Shallows and miseries shadows from the cross,
ecco men and dull copernican sun.

The vision of the restoration of a "human universe" rides
enthusiastically on the tide and disperses the miseries and
shadows of tradition-bound "ecco men." When this occurs,

Our attention is simpler
The salts and minerals of the earth return . . .

"Attention" is an important word for Olson and implies
a state of complete fidelity to the objectist stance,[9] a state of
absorption so complete that no room remains for abstractions or references. In attempting to explain "attention" at
the home of the Gratwicks, Olson claimed it as "the source
of our very existence as human beings" and then whimsi-
cally illustrated the point with tigers: "They don't have
anything else to do! They are not involved with attention.
They are attention." In short, when one pays attention, the
"experience outside is definitely identical with the experience inside."[10]

"The K," then, optimistically marks the start of a new direction for Olson, for Truman, for the nation and ultimately for civilization in quest of that state of attention that
is possible only when man is totally involved with "that with
which he is most familiar"—a "human universe."

Something of this state of attention charges the strange
but powerful poem "The Moebius Strip," which, with all its
sensual, struggling energy, gives off the final impression
of self-contained, active absorption. The title itself, alluding to the finite boundlessness that characterizes the topology of the moebius strip, provides a novel space-time
terrain for the activities of the figures who populate it. The
terrain, the figures, the poem itself are all as topologically
continuous and connected as the surface of the strip on
which they move:

in round,
of viscera, of legs

> of turned-out hip and glance, bound
> each to other, nested eggs
> of elements in trance.

The universe of this "Moebius Strip" disallows discontinuity, which distracts human "attention." It possesses an epistemological integrity that permits its inhabitants the same total alertness of the tiger. They do not *pay* attention to their world and their physicality; they *are* that attention.

"Trinacria" is an invitation to come out into the open field. Fighting "behind a shield" is a sterile, "separate" activity that rejects the mythic energies available from "dream." If one's attention is limited to what is going on "outside" to the neglect of the significant goings on within, then he possesses a reality that is only "half slain." Whitehead's epistemological notions of "causal efficacy" and "presentational immediacy" lie behind the poem. It is not enough to visually apprehend the world ("presentational immediacy"); one must also apprehend it bodily, too ("causal efficacy"). As Olson himself states in *Proprioception*, "one's life is informed from and by one's own literal body," which provides "the DEPTH implicit in physical being" (*AP*, 18). The warrior who blocks off his bodily depth dimension and fights only with the "sword" of presentational immediacy will be "whirled by sons of self" and will win no "fleece." The proper martial stance is to

> Join sword and shield, yield
> Neither ground, contend ...

This, of course, is the attitude of "attention" that comes when the sword of "presentational immediacy" functions in tandem with the shield of "causal efficacy—what happens outside conjoined with what happens within.

"Attention" is given brilliant dramatic treatment in the bullfight poem called simply "This." The scene is an arena. We are surrounded by "a crazy trumpet / of a band, few / people, sloppy / cowboys picadors matadors bulls" and are asked to regard "*out there, on that dirt, in front*" nothing less than our "existence." The poem presents the bullfight as "an instant declaration of that which you know is all / that constitutes both what you are and what is going on at all time." The bullfight is the act of "attention" itself. The bull, like the attentive tiger, "*is / involved*," but oddly enough he is described as less an "*animal*" than man. This lesser animality probably refers to the fact that the bull's experience is "so very clear"; it is not clouded, as is the men's, by fear. Bull and man do, nevertheless, share a visceral commonality:

> *the men (the man) so much more*
> *animal, so*
> *aware, their*
> *courage (fear) so*
> *very clear, so very much the reason why*
> *we too are*
> *involved, why*
> *we, here, . . .*

Man and bull feel the attentiveness that "plain danger" brings: "*this bull and this man (these men) can / kill / one another.*"

In letter number 5 to Robert Creeley from Campeche, Olson had a number of criticisms to make of Pound. "So much of Ez is, the 19th century stance: PROTEST," he writes, adding,

> (Dahlberg is the funny man, of same biz: they both wld love to have been, who was it, Lousie 14th, 'l'état, c'est moi'? what burns me, is, they never speak, in their slash at the State or the Economy, basically, for anyone but themselves. And thus, it is Bohemianism. (*ML*, 29)

Olson, with his "special view" of history, naturally rejected the social protest stance, Bohemian or no, arguing that

> the substances of history now useful lie outside, under, right here, anywhere but in the direct continuum of society as we have had it (of the State, same, of the Econ-

omy, same, of the Politicks: Ez is traitor as Dante was, to Florence. (*ML*, 14)

He had voiced a somewhat similar exasperation at the archeological "Establishment" who laughed at him because they were only interested to "discover more abt the economic & political life of the ancient Maya," while Olson considered himself "an aestheticist." At any rate, Pound betrayed Florence, Olson thought, sharing the now-familiar view that the elder Pound sold out art to economics and politics.

A poetic, custard-pie version of this contretemps with Pound takes place in "Issue, Mood" in which Olson concedes that his thoughts

> still go funny, in the face of
> him on money
> > like
> people say, right in the face of
> (prat): not chuman not chuman not
> hoomin

Pound on money is not only "not chuman," but is as comically bizarre as a pratfall, a pie in the face, or a pun. With the authority of having been a Roosevelt "newt" dealer in the forties, Olson asks his all-too-theoretical "Poet-Economist" friend,

> > Comes
> the revolution, does
> this laborer lose
> this labor of his arm?
> > Or this Lake,
>
> Maracaibo, its
> oil?

The realities are oil and the works of man's hand not revolutions, movements, or abstractions like Society. After all,

who's wrong, what's
society.
      and who
be thee? be thee
one of the Innocents?

Hardly. Pound speaks for Bohemia. But perhaps worse, he has degenerated to

           the habit
to look to society to make it
new.

    bah.

Olson once defined mythology as "the kosmos inside a human being," adding the corollary that "it is with EROS that mythology is concerned. Which amounts to saying that as a psyche man is only an order comparable to kosmos when he or she is in love." A potentially romantic premise indeed, but Olson's actual intent is to reaffirm Carl Jung's view that we should "accord the pysche the same validity as the empirical world, and to admit that the former has just as much 'reality' as the latter."[11] This being so, Olson feels that we should expect "on the personal level ... imperatives as fierce as those we know in the interchange of energy and mass" (*SVH*, 55). "The Cause, the Cause," takes an instance of a lover dominated by one of the most fierce imperatives ever recorded—Othello's "cause" for murdering Desdemona—and uses it with Jungian ingenuity to unfold once again his favorite theme: "Man is estranged from that with which he is most familiar" (*SVH*, 14).

The estrangement here is not cultural, nor epistemological, but psychological—man artificially "halved," his conscicous self divided against his unconscious. The notion is, of course, Jung's. There are two sides to the personality: the "logos," which refers to the masculine clarity of consciousness and reason; and the "anima," which al-

ludes to the existence of a feminine figure in the unconscious with its deeper introspection or ecstatic experience.
In the healthy, integrated psyche both logos and anima
coexist, demonstrating the kind of Heraclitean union of
opposites that Olson believed to be the essence of reality
and art:

> I mean, discords, The discordant, The want of agree-
> ment. The want of concord or harmony. Variance, dis-
> sension, contention, dissonance. Contest. The *agon* as
> well as the *pathos* and the *epiphany* . . . The shift, from
> sorrow to joy.[12]

The opening of the poem characterizes the union of logos
and anima (perhaps because "the method be / new") by
means of the "rods and cones of, a pigeon's or, a rabbit's /
eye" (pigeons and rabbits are standard in the iconography
of Venus and thus appropriately suggest something of the
quality of love's vision). Rods are those minute parts of the
visual anatomy that are functional only at low levels of il-
lumination and, like the anima, extend the range of sen-
sitivity despite their crudeness in discerning details. Cones,
on the other hand, correspond to the logos in the sense
that their function is to pick up fine details, make dis-
criminations and detect colors. Accordingly, the poem
later speaks of "*his* sort of looking out by cones" and "*her*
rods," re-emphasizing the distinction between the masculine and feminine principles involved.

That any psyche consists of both masculine and
feminine qualities and that gender is arbitrarily determined by a "hair's" difference ("Made male by one point
short majority") is a notion that the poem particularly
exploits. It depicts the psyche as a kind of battleground in
which logos and anima (masculine and feminine) contend
as warring lovers:

>   the nightmare is
> the day's ambiguous responses, her
> harassments, his

flying off, . . .
      his
watchings . . .
      her
subjects so badly introduced, her rods, her
in the eye, in the eye of his will, her
multiple withholdings, her
not at all dumb dance, her measurings

How ingeniously Olson weaves an accurate assessment of Desdemona, as she actually behaves in the play, while simultaneously depicting an equally accurate contention between the logos and the anima! In either case the outcome is the same:

                              he

   smothered her

Why this is tragic in the drama is no problem, but what is the nature of the tragedy psychically? The logos smothered the anima

    because he could not free his half self from her likeness, carried (jealous) buried, you can say, and no more mirroring her—no, not at all, in fact a she, initiate with himself alone, another creature concealed in him—a female male to him his confusion

Othello-logos, confused to distraction by the "female male" in him, seeks to "free" himself from that buried half, that other "creature concealed in him," his unconscious, the anima. The tragedy, however, is not so much the "smothering" of that anima, but that Othello should have ever come to "this queer juncture" that "he should find himself a double." In other words, the tragedy is the dissolution of integrity that prompts the artificial feeling of "doubleness" that, in turn, initiates the alienation of the anima by the logos. Olson is simply documenting his version of the Fall of Man, which turns out to be the "birth of discourse"—that moment when the estrangement from

that with which man is most familiar (the anima, the unconscious) occurs. Indeed, Olson's Othello smothers his
anima half

> for half love of another
> Eve.

But there is another half to the tragedy. It "repeats itself
in inverse, . . . for woman, too, is joined & sundered, returned . . . to mono-beast, she too conceals a brother
[and] . . .

> again,
> murder, another
> murder

The feminine anima can also seek freedom from her masculine "half self" and the brutal destruction of psychic integrity is the same.

What, then, is the "cause"? The poem answers that
question with one word: "difference." These murders of
psychic integrity result from the inability to live with difference. Opposition should not be regarded as an abnor-
mal state of affairs; it is quintessential normality. Reality,
whether outside in the "kosmos" or inside the psyche, is by
its nature, "dissension, contention, dissonance" and should
be appreciated as such. When it is not, the place of man
and woman, their psychic Eden, becomes "dirtied . . .
fouled."

In 1963 during a symposium in Vancouver that included Creeley, Duncan, and Ginsberg, Olson responded
to the query "What is 'history'?" by reading his poem
"Place; & Names." It is an obscure and poetically pedes-
trian poem, and many might share Ginsberg's spontaneous
reaction to Olson's reading of it: "I don't understand what
you're saying." [13] Nevertheless, it is a statement that is
central to Olson's commitment to the space-time premise.

The subject is "place," and Olson seeks a nonhistorical,
nongeographical definition of the word that might appro-

priately address what he calls the "Isness of Cosmos." "Isness" is a coinage comparable to "suchness" in Taoism: that is, "that which exists through itself." Thus, the "Isness of Cosmos" is the alternative to a cosmos that is the construction of intellectual reflection. In essence, it is the "human universe." Experiencing and then naming "place" are activities of the creative artist who avails himself of "nominative power—& landshaft / experience" to accomplish the feat. "Place" so "named" must retain a commonality to all men. The force of the common can be retained, Olson explains elsewhere, by "not falling for realism, or the false particularism of the autobiographical" (*LO*, 82). Actual events and specific place-names will not accomplish commonality. (We may recall Olson's chiding of Rainer Gerhardt for his "false particularism" in trying to "lift" Europe by a bare listing of the names of cities). It is not a matter of accurate data, true description, nor exact registration. The commonality that "place" seeks is the knowledge that one takes in through the pores or with the body. It is won through causal efficacy that Olson will later link with the collective unconscious and thus to mythic truth. You know a "place" because you are there; it is that "with which you are most familiar"; it is a precinct of the "human universe."

"Place; & Names," in fact, asks that we regard

>these places or names
> ...as parts of the body, common, & capable
> therefore of having cells which decant
> total experience—

The method by which these cells decant is story-telling; that is, the total experience of the cell is gathered into a "fiction" that holds more truth than the most exhaustive reportage. Olson justifies the linkage of "cell" to "story" by appeal to "Duncan's Law." This Law originates in a letter that Robert Duncan wrote to Olson in which he used the word *histology* to embrace the notions of "cell" and "story" as expressions of the same thing. In Herodotus's sense of *'istorin* ("to find out for one's self"), history is as immediately and comprehensively known as one knows the "cells" of his body. Both "story" (in Herodotus's sense) and "cell" therefore "decant / total experience." "After all," Olson points out,

> Herodotus goes around and finds out everything he can find out, and then he tells a story. It's one of the reasons why I trust him more than, say, Thucydides, who basically is reporting an event.[14]

Story versus report, myth versus fact, "place" versus New York City—these are the distinctions that characterize the difference between the "Isness" of space-time and the generalities of the "universe of discourse." They suggest why the "complementarity of / cosmos" must be understood to mean "complementary to individual or private . . . and not to cities or events in the way it has, in / a mistaken secondary way, been / understood."

"A Discrete Gloss" is a lesson in perception that finally matures at its close into a full-blown attack (couched in the "precisions of Mayan art") against "discourse." It opens with the speaker standing by a beach (presumably in Campeche) cataloguing the discrete objects that fall under his vision: "the tide, the number 9 . . . creation . . . this church . . . this slaughter house behind it." The experience prompts this speculation:

> whatever sits outside you is
> by what difference what
> you also are . . .
> In what sense is
> what happens before the eye
> so very different from
> what actually goes on within . . .

This perceptual conundrum hinges on Olson's familiar distinction between "inner" and "outer" things that he previously treated in "Trinacria." The answer to the query is thus predictable: "what happens before the eye" and "what actually goes on within" are complementary epistemological events. "I am not able to satisfy myself," Olson wrote in the "Human Universe,"

> that these so-called inner things ["dreams ... thoughts ... desires, sins, hopes, fears, faiths, loves"] are so separable from the objects, persons, events which are the content of them. (*HU*, 10)

Since the notion is originally Whitehead's, his elaboration of the phenomenon is helpful:

> When we register in consciousness our visual perception of a grey stone, something more than bare sight is meant. The "stone" has a reference to its past, when it could be used as a missile, if small enough, or as a seat if large enough.... But we all know that the mere sight involved ... is the sight of a grey shape contemporaneous with the percipient.... Thus the mere sight is confined to the illustration of the geometrical perspective relatedness, of a certain contemporary spatial region, to the percipient.[15]

"Mere sight" or, for that matter, mere sensory perception in its broadest sense, is what "A Discrete Gloss" militates against. It does not exist except as an abstraction. "Your eye, the wanderer, sees more," the poem insists. It sees:

                    what happens
    somewhere else: where, say, the sea
    is more sea, and men
    do not take Saturday Sunday off, arguing
    they need to clean the gurry, a boat
    takes that much drying, that much
    sun.

Experience from within, the memory and the emotions, enriches and shapes the visual sensations from without. A stone is enhanced by our unconscious knowledge that it could serve as a missile or a chair. The work ethic of Campechian fishermen is superimposed upon a recollected field of New England industriousness. We place grey stones or dryng boats within a context composed of our unconscious depth sensibility—fears, dreams, memories, hunches, prejudices—or at least we hope we do, for

> When the field of focus
> is not admitted as the point is,
> what loss!

In other words, as Olson expresses the point in "The Human Universe":

> If man chooses to treat external reality any differently than as part of his own process, in other words as anything other than relevant to his own inner life, then he will . . . use it just as exactly as he has used it now for too long, for arbitrary and willful purposes which, in their effects, not only change the face of nature, but actually arrest and divert her force. (*HU*, 11)

One culture that managed not to divert nature's force is the Maya who still (despite the plague of "discourse" elsewhere) "can seize / as the sun seizes . . . can take some human thigh bone . . . and with a stone tool carve such likeness on it . . . as the man you draw / was Quetzalcoatl more a sea-horse than himself." So powerful were the Mayan creative acts (because they twinned nature to their own processes) that they were able to make "gorging nature at her blackest root / a silly starer too."

The culture of the Maya, as we have learned from "The Kingfishers," suggests the character of a new age of man:

> The day of man returns in your precisions, kin
> (ahau, katun), the force
> of force where force forever is

The Mayan hieroglyphs themselves contain nature's force and testify that, indeed, "Man is no creature of his own discourse." To the contrary, he is a creature of Nature's force attuned to *his own* processes. For this reason

these boats dry in colours only he
had an eye for. And it says, it says here
in the face of everything it says
this, is the more exact

There are more poems and more sides to Olson's
energetic quest to restore a "human universe" in *Archaeologist of Morning*. There is the raw, brutal sexuality of
the "O'Ryan" sequence that vividly exposes yet another,
darker manifestation of attentive "isness." There is the
controversial translation from the Hurrian and Hittite,
"The Song of Ullikumi," which Olson read at Spoleto,
Italy, in honor of Pound, and which Marjorie Perloff takes
heavily to task for its nonprojective repetitiveness.[16] There
are the pithy whimsicalities of "Asymptotes" ("yup, our
disgraces are / our Graces ... say, have you got a match, /
Prometheus?") and the brisk parodies of "The Morning
News." There is even some Olsonian demythologizing in
"Christmas," in which the divinity of Christ is negatively
contrasted to the purer, healthier picture of "a man
standing / in desire in the / Jordan, with green / banks on
either / side, a naked man."

The volume is a kind of notebook full of varied poetic
markings that, despite their apparent eccentricities, their
exotic subjects, their arresting forms, their sense of having
been scribbled on the run by an impatient sage, nevertheless reveal in their accumulation a swelling discernible
coherence that confirms our suspicions that Olson's power
derives not from the eclectic quirkiness of its practices, nor
even the bulldozer energy with which it plows syllables across line, but from the integrity of the selections it makes
from the bewildering chaos of Olson's voracious reading
and equally voracious experiences. It is as if that tidal
obedience that governs his life also governs what sticks to
his poetic ribs. His single encompassing notion of a
"human universe" draws materials akin to its aims like a
magnet and these become the materials of the poems,
which themselves integrate to the wholeness of a corpus.
This volume is one such corpus. Another is *The Maximus
Poems*.

160 THE POETRY OF CHARLES OLSON

NOTES

1. See Ann Charters, *Olson/Melville: A Study in Affinity* (Berkeley, Calif.: Oyez, 1968), p. 84.
2. The passage from "The Present Is Prologue" continues: "And the writing and acts which I find bear on the present job are (1) from Homer back, not forward; . . ." (*AP*, 40).
3. *Archaeologist of Morning* is unpaginated and so parenthetical page citations are impractical. For the most part, the poems are discrete and quoted passages are reasonably easy to find.
4. "Sense-perception of the contemporary world is accompanied by perception of the 'withness' of the body. It is this witness that makes the body the starting point for our knowledge of the circumambient world. We find here our direct knowledge of 'causal efficacy'" (Alfred Whitehead, *Process and Reality* [New York: Macmillan Co., 1929], p. 125).
5. Olson, "Notes for the Proposition: Man is Prospective," *Boundary 2* 2 (Fall 1973/Winter 1974): 2.
6. Ibid., p. 4.
7. Charters, *Olson/Melville*, pp. 84–85.
8. Ibid., p. 9.
9. A sense of what Olson meant by "attention" comes out in this dialogue with his neighbor, Herbert A. Kenny: "Herb, we're talking something that's gone out in practically our life. . . . Each day a man went to work he was in danger. . . . But there's none of that sense of, of that you're up against the whole of nature, right? . . . it is the nature of perception, of attention, yes. Which is a spiritual condition. You could put it, intensity. I mean, the amount of slackness today, the laziness, the lackness, the limpness, is all in the fact that you don't *need* attention any more, you don't need your perceptions any more" ('I know men for whom everything matter': Charles Olson in Conversation with Herbert A. Kenny," *Olson* 1 (Spring 1974): 30. 1974): 30.
10. Olson, "Under the Mushroom: The Gratwick Highlands Tape," *Olson* 3 (Spring 1975): 49.
11. Carl Jung, "Commentary," in *The Secret of the Golden Flower*, trans. Richard Wilhelm, rev. ed. (New York: Harcourt, Brace & World, Inc., 1962), p. 130.
12. Charters, *Olson/Melville*, p. 88.
13. Olson, "On 'History,'" *Olson* 4 (Fall, 1975): 42.
14. Ibid., pp. 42–43.
15. Whitehead, *Process and Reality*, pp. 184–85.
16. Marjorie Perloff, "Charles Olson and the 'Inferior Predecessors': 'Projective Verse' Revisited," *ELH* 40 (Summer 1973): 305.

[6]
The Maximus Poems

H. K.: Well, Charles, what do you
        think the future of
        Gloucester on Cape Ann will
        be?

C. O.: [Pauses.] An image of creation
        and of human life for the rest
        of the life of the species.
        —"'I know men for whom
           everything matters'"

The Maximus Poems joins such earlier indigenous efforts as the *Columbiad, Song of Myself, The Cantos, The Bridge*, and *Paterson* in the quest for an "American equivalent of the epic."[1] From its opening dedication to Creeley ("the figure of Outward") to the unleashing of its closing mythic obscurities, its intentions are unabashedly grand. The epigraph "All my life I've heard / one makes many," for example, while actually a fragment of conversation picked up in the Black Mountain College kitchen, serves as perhaps a deliberately pretentious challenge to *Paterson*'s ambitious program: " . . . *in distinctive terms; by multiplication a reduction to one*."[2] Maximus, the hero-genius of Gloucester, arises in the first lines with calculated epic majesty from a splendidly magnificent covert "in the blood / jewels & miracles" like "a metal hot from boiling water" (*M*, 1). From the start expectations are tuned high.

Maximus, like his predecessor Dr. Paterson, is a gigantic, omniscient extension of his creator; he is observer, historian, social critic, correspondent, mail carrier, voyeur, and poet. He communicates to Gloucester and to himself in a series of "letters" that constitute the poem's prevailing structure. While each "letter" possesses an integrity, a projective coherence, of its own, it demonstrates directly and by implication organic connections to the others. For those familiar with projective form, the mode is topological, but for the uninitiated, the "letter" device only draws attention to the familiar critical charges leveled at earlier attempts at the long form: how does the long poem or sequence achieve an overall unity? How does *Maximus*, an alleged literary entity, distinguish itself from merely thematically related collections such as Olson's own *The Distances* or even *Archaeologist of Morning*?

Olson was sensitive to these concerns as well as to the fact that as epic pioneer he was contributing to a frontier already half-tamed. His problem was not the same as his "inferior predecessors" (*LO*, 132), Pound and Williams, who had earlier first broken American epic ground; he felt compelled to demonstrate that despite its obvious debts to *Paterson* and *The Cantos, Maximus* nevertheless extended the "push" beyond their "half-successes" (*ML*, 28).

The demonstration was not easy. On the face of it *Maximus* seems enormously derivative. Olson's theme of modern man's estrangement from "that with which he is most familiar" seems perilously reminiscent of *Paterson*'s evocation of the cultural "divorce" that characterizes modern life. Both epics discover their respective estrangements and divorces in language. Both Williams's "divorce" theme and Pound's economic obsessions appear to foreshadow Olson's diatribes against "mu-sick" and "pejorocracy" (*M*, 3) that suffuse *Maximus*. Even in minor details the debts are evident. At one point in *Paterson* Williams characterizes his enterprise as "a basket,"[3] a container for particulars, which surely is the suggestion that prompts *Maximus*'s series of "nests," "kylixes," and other containers that are constructed and then filled with the "hay and cotton struts,/ of street-pickings, wharves, weeds / you carry in, my bird . . ." (*M*, 3). Even Olson's persistent concern for "place," so splendidly elaborated by Ed Dorn,[4] seems anticipated by Williams's observation that "place is the only reality, the true core of the universal."[5] These parallels,

added to the patent kinship of the epic heroes, Dr. Paterson and Maximus, lend some plausibility to Marjorie Perloff's opinion that Olson's poesy is a pale imitation rather
than a creative advance over Pound and Williams.[6]

Olson's claim for innovation rests in *Maximus*'s success in
making "historical material . . . free for forms now" (*ML*,
26). He intended his epic to demonstrate with "absolute
clarity, that, time, is done, as effect of work in hand" (*ML*,
28). Pound, he pointed out, tried to defeat historical time
with "the beak of his ego . . . [turning] time into what we
must now have, space & its live air" (*ML*, 27). According to
Olson, Pound's "single emotion breaks all down to his
equals or inferiors (so far as I can see only two, possibly,
are admitted, by him, to be his betters—Confucius, &
Dante. Which assumption, that there are intelligent men
he can outtalk, is beautiful because it destroys historical
time, and thus creates the methodology of the Cantos"
(*ML*, 26).

James Joyce, Olson continues, attempted an alternative
method: "he tried to get at the problem by running one
language into another so as to create a universal language
of the unconscious" (*ML*, 27). Williams, however, offers
the "primary contrast." Williams "HAS an emotional system which is capable of extensions & comprehensions the
ego-system . . . is not" (*ML*, 27). Where Williams fails, however, is in "making his substance historical of one city (the
Joyce deal)." By doing so, he "lets time roll him under as
Ez does not, and thus, so far as what is the most important,
methodology, contributes nothing" (*ML*, 28).

But is not making the "substance historical of one city"
precisely what Olson did by anchoring his *Maximus* to the
city of Gloucester? Not, at least, in Olson's view. Williams
selected a single city to assure intimacy with the local even
though he did not consider the local an end in itself. His
aim was "to be both local (all art is local) and at the same
time to surmount that restriction by climbing to the universal in all art."[7] In Olson's judgment, Williams's position
was time-bound. His commitment to the particulars of an
historical Paterson as the substance of his poem incarcer-

ated that work in the prison of "past history" rather than an historical "now." Williams's method, laudable as it was in its focus on particulars, simply did not succeed in rendering "historical material . . . free for forms now" (*ML*, 26).

Olson rendered his Gloucester timeless with sweeping claims. When asked by Gregory Corso why he was writing about a city that was going to disappear, he replied, "I consider her a redeemable flower that will be a monstrance forever, of not a city but of City."[8] Williams had chosen Paterson for the site of his epic on the basis of its formal and geographical convenience; he conceivably might have been as successful with Camden or Buffalo had he grown up near those cities. Gloucester, however, was for Olson a "monstrance," "City," and, as he once confided to his neighbor Herbert Kenny, "an image of creation and of human life for the rest of the life of the species." Gloucester had *intrinsic* significance, a point Olson amplified for Kenny:

> Because by being so retrograde at an enormous progressive time, yet having been the absolute "Siracusa" or whatever was the first of the great colonies of Greece. . . . I regard Gloucester as the final movement of the earth's people, the great migratory thing, . . . The migratory act of man ended in Gloucester. And I think the migratory act of man is the fillet of the rose, is the fire of the energy patterns.[9]

As the "final movement of the earth's people," Gloucester is indeed not merely "a city" but "City" itself, resolutely present in the here-and-now. Considering his locus in that light, Olson felt assured he could evade the illusion of "past time," as Williams before him had not.

The specific methodology for evading "past time," according to Olson, was to get "rid of nomination" (*ML*, 26). Nomination locks historical material into time and, as an alternative, Olson suggests searching for "etymon. The right word. The root. Not at all the usages, the behaviors of the word, but the actual thing that *it* is." The discovery of the etymon is one's exit from the "universe of discourse," for it brings back "the familiar." "And that thing in itself," Olson continues, "is where we really have a chance to put our hand out and grab hold of something. Otherwise we're simply getting caught in the event either of the society, which is one form of what's boringly called history, or the event of ourselves, which is also that damn boring thing called personal history."[10]

Etymon, then, is the means to avoid the illusion of "past history" that nomination apparently sponsors. It is a strategy that makes "historical material ... free for forms now," acknowledging the fact that "there's no place that the past can take place except right now.... The past has no other existence. It has only existence as it is right present."[11] Pound and Williams apparently failed to rid their work of nomination. As Creeley explains it, "Williams' dilemma in *Paterson*, in terms of this context, was that he was straddling. He was trying to make up a city. He was involved with histology, but then he'd get involved with concepts prior to looking."[12] Looking, hearing, smelling, and moving (all activities emphasized in *Maximus*) are present acts—modes of "finding out for one's self" among the materials directly before the senses. What finally distinguishes *Maximus* from its predecessors is this one significant feature: it is truly an epic committed to the methodology of Herodotus's *'istorin*, finding out for one's self and rendering the results as present "story" rather than historical "report." Proof of the non-Herodotean method of Pound and Williams resides in the datability of their efforts. " ... i don't think Ez's toucan works after 1971," Olson wrote to Creeley.

> ... the materials of history which he has found useful are not at all of use (not Bill's, despite the more apparent homogeneity: date 1917, not only did Yurrup (West, Cento, Renaissance) go, but such blueberry America as Bill presents (Jersey dump-smoke covering same) also WENT (that is, Bill, with all respect, don't know fr nothing abt what a city *is*)
>
> the which says this: that the substances of history now useful lie outside, under, right here, anywhere but in

the direct continuum of society as we have had it (of the
State, same, of the Economy, same, of Politicks: Ez is
traitor as Dante was, to Florence: the difference of F to
USA is not difference at all, other than, the passage of
time & time's dreary accumulations by repetition. (*ML*,
30)

Maximus's heroic entrance as the epic opens would seem
to dispel any fear that we might be in for "dreary accumulations," time's or anyone else's. Our hero is both grandly
oracular and, like Olson's Mayan neighbors in Lerma, "hot
for the world . . . hot to get it down the way it was—the way
it is" (*HU*, 15). As a principle of methodology, "was" means
"is" for this protagonist who "obeys the figures of / the
present dance" [italics added].

After this brief introduction of Maximus, the poem
proper opens with the announcement of a quest ("the
thing you're after / may lie around the bend / of the nest"),
a suggestion of methodology ("time slain"), and an amal-
gamation of the instruments to be used on the quest ("the
bird! the bird! / And there! (strong) thrust, the mast!
flight"). The bird immediately emerges as a figure of creative discovery, nervously gathering the stray particulars of
the city to furnish its nest. The "nest" itself connects the
creative movement of the bird with the beginning of an
epic voyage upon a ship, suggesting, as it does, the crow's
nest of "the mast." We soon learn that the ship's prow is
adorned (guided) by the "lady of good voyage" (*M*, 2),
whose

> . . . underpart is, though stemmed, uncertain
> is, as sex is, as moneys are, facts!

The "facts," we are told, must "be dealt with, as the sea is,"
that is, they "must / be played by . . . the ear" (*M*, 2).

All the familiar elements of Olson's métier are present
here. The "lady of good voyage" guides the epic enterprise
according to some uncertain obedience to "the demand"
(*M*, 2, 8) in spite of "the deathly mu-sick" (*M*, 8) that inces-
santly seeks to drown it out. The ship itself rides on "facts,"

particulars, which must be dealt with not analytically, not historically, but "by ear" (*M*, 2), as things spontaneously confronted and heard for the first time. The old familiar curse of the "universe of discourse" is now objectified in "billboards" and "spray-gunned" silences, and even "sound itself is neoned in" (*M*, 2). The goal of the quest is obvious from the outset; it is the familiar—facts, unadulterated by the linguistic static of "mu-sick"that reduces the once-proud glory of man to

> ... a man slumped,
> attentionless,
> against pink shingles

Since "love is form" (*M*, 1), the deterioration of contemporary forms means also the deterioration of love:

> love is not easy
> but how shall you know,
> New England, now
> that pejorocracy is here
>   (*M*, 3)

Pejorocracy, the political, economic and social aspect of "mu-sick," undermines the dignity of labor and craftsmanship:

> how shall you strike,
> o swordsman, the blue-red back
> when, last night, your aim
> was mu-sick, mu-sick, mu-sick
> And not the cribbage game?
>   (*M*, 3)

The appeal is clear. Values and practices must be recast to fit "facts" rather than the illusions of "mu-sick" and "pejorocracy":

> (o Gloucester-man
> weave
> your birds and fingers

> new . . .
> o kill kill kill kill kill
> those
> who advertise you
>   out)
>   (*M*, 3-4)

There are, of course, other forces besides advertising that obscure those "facts" of reality with which we should be "most familiar." Letter 2, "Maximus, to Gloucester," addresses itself to them. It presents a chiaroscuro of the city, arranging the whites and blacks into an emphatic moral tableau. The brilliant reflected light of the houses only emphasizes the hidden darknesses of Gloucester's past:

> they hid, or tried to hide, the fact the cargo their ships
>   brought back
> was black (the Library, too, possibly so founded
>   (*M*, 5)

Illusory surfaces hide other secret facts:

> . . . it's the doctor knows
> what the parents don't know. Or the wife doesn't
> of the husband, or the husband, of the other. Sins,
>
> they still call them, and let
> pejorocracy thrive. Only the lady
>
> has got it straight. She looks
> as the best of my people look
> in one direction, her direction . . .
>   (*M*, 6)

Here is epistemological duplicity sanctioned by the concept of "sins," and it is Gloucester's willingness to institutionalize illusion that nurtures pejorocracy. Maximus's alternative morality thrives in the "lady of good voyage," who alone "has got it straight," manifesting her integrity by the unwavering direction of her gaze. She is the embodiment of Whitehead's "blind perceptivity"—that obedience to "what we are in the hands of"—to which

Olson relentlessly committed his trust. She arouses "the best of my people" by rejecting the "false future" of "mu-sick" and bearing witness instead to a faith in the "elements men stand in the midst of." She is the holy mother of ob-jectism, and her "demand" draws to her that perennial group of stalwarts who reside in all cultures, those which Olson later dubs "polis" (*M*, 10,11,20,24,26,28,64):

> While she stares, out of her painted face,
> no matter the deathly mu-sick, the
> > demand
> will arouse
> some of these men and women
> > > (*M*, 8)

One of the most lyrical "letters" of *Maximus* is the "tansy" sequence, number 3, but its pastoral veneer is deceptive. In fact, it is a passionate indictment of all mu-sick-makers, "those who use words cheap" (*M*, 9), and apparently has as its model King Lear's moving appeal on the heath for di-vine vengeance upon the corruptors of civilization:

> Let the great gods,
> That keep this dreadful pother o'er our heads,
> Find out their enemies now. Tremble, thou wretch,
> That hast within thee undivulged crimes, . . .
> > (3.2. 49–52)

Tansy is an aromatic and medicinal flower, and it is put to the task here of hygienically eliminating the "smell / of all owners" (*M*, 9) from Gloucester. As pastoral avenger, tansy wars against duplicity in all its forms. Like the "lady of good voyage," it insists upon the restoration of cultural integrity even to the essential workings of the language it-self: a word should "mean not a single thing the least more than / what it does mean" (*M*, 11). Tansy is prime. Tansy is the blazon of "root person in root place" (*M*, 12) and so naturally is employed as an antibody to

> that mu-sick (the trick
> of corporations, newspapers, slick magazines, movie

houses,
the ships, even the wharves, absentee-owned
                    (*M*, 10)

that adulterates the natural, pastoral simplicity of

            that lovely hour
the Waiting Station, 5 o'clock, the Magnolia bus,
Al Levy
on duty . . .

                            (*M*, 11)

Tansy picks up the faith of the "lady of good voyage" from Letter 2 in hopes of arousing the small "coherence" (*M*, 11) of citizens who make up "polis" to militate against the "slaver" of the owners who "would keep you off the sea, would keep you local" (*M*, 12). Indeed, the "local" is not in Gloucester the virtue it was in Paterson. For Olson, Gloucester is etymon.

In the "Songs of Maximus" the complaints are the same but the tone is more intimate, personal. The songs are soliloquies from amid the "gurry," echoing the frustrations of an earlier protagonist (who "knows not 'seems'"), Hamlet:

    words, words, words
            (*M*, 13)

The words Maximus laments are the message from "dirty postcards" (*M*, 13), actually the advertising placards in street-cars. They are, of course, visual "mu-sick" and they have "invaded, appropriated, outraged, all senses / including the mind" (*M*, 13). Even Maximus is "covered / with the gurry of it" (*M*, 13) and asks

                where
shall we go from here, what can we do
when even public conveyances
sing?

                            (*M*, 13)

One suggestion that comes to his mind is to count the

"blessings" of "difficulties" (*M*, 14). In Olson's ascetic view there is virtue in the natural obstacles and challenges of everyday life that contemporary progress, with its "mu-sick" and "Congoleum" have all but blotted out. The "leak in the faucet / which makes of the sink time" (*M*, 14), the expediency of mending the toilet with "paper clips," the "holes" in the shoes, the "fly gaping"—these ingenious ac-commodations to the mundane "elements men stand in the midst of" (*M*, 6) are celebrated as victories over pejorocracy, and they inspire the counsel:

> "In the midst of plenty, walk
> as close to
> bare
>   In the face of sweetness,
> piss
>   In the time of goodness,
> go side, go
> smashing . . .
> In the land of plenty, have
> nothing to do with it . . ."
>   (*M*, 14–15)

Such cultural recalcitrance is not bred of mere perver-sity. It emerges from a primal source deep beneath the gurry, from the distant recollection of some Innisfree of the Unconscious where a "house made of mud & wattles," innocent of Congoleum, surely exists. It emerges from an earlier "polis" where Nike's graceful movements testify to her congruence with Nature. It emerges from the awe of seeing a living specimen of man's ultimate ancestor, the primitive coelacanth, said to have existed 300 million years ago. These testaments to the grace and power of authentic "human motion" (*M*,15) are thrown in brutal contrast against the "mu-sick" that has "greased" and "lulled" (*M*, 13) the modern senses into a fatal, unproductive ease. It is not ease, but the natural difficulties of life that give it its integrity, and that is why authentic verse thrives best with need:

> you sing, you
> who also

> wants
>> (*M*, 16)

Vincent Ferrini, poet and editor of the Gloucester literary quarterly *Four Winds*, was Olson's friend, although the viciousness of Olson's attack on issue #3 of that short-lived publication (immortalized in "Letter 5" of *Maximus*) might seem to belie that fact. The entire editoral orientation of *Four Winds* offended Olson, and he held Ferrini responsible for what he considered simply one more outlet for "mu-sick." The venom of his attack in *Maximus* demonstrates the absolute nature of Olson's priorities: principle preceded friendship. The editorial principles he had so forcefully insisted upon with Cid Corman (*LO*, 2–11) transcended all nonliterary matters. "These new Maxies rough up Vinc considerably—I was shocked by both the choice of things, & their putting together . . ." he wrote to Corman and later included in *Maximus*. "Hold his hand (tho I don't think he deserves forgiveness) I just hate that the necessities (at least as I take them are bigger than we are only I hate it, that he had to go & get caught in the wringer" (*LO*, 124; *M*, 41).

Simply put, Olson's complaint against Ferrini and his magazine was that they were "culture mongers" (*M*, 18). *Four Winds* lost its integrity by straying beyond Gloucester's "limits of literacy" (*M*, 17), which Olson defined as "The habit of newsprint / (plus possibly the National Geographic)" (*M*, 17). Olson was not putting down the intelligence of the citizens of Gloucester; he was merely acknowledging the fact that "Limits / are what any of us / are inside of" (*M*, 17). Because Ferrini had deliberately placed himself outside those limits, Olson eventually concluded that

> It's no use.
> There is no place we can meet.
> You have left Gloucester.
> You are not there, you are anywhere

where there are little magazines
will publish you
(M, 25)

Olson's point was not merely that *Four Winds* ignored
local particulars ("Nor assuage yrself I use the local as a
stick to beat you" [*M*, 20]); it is that like all contemporary
"mu-sick" *Four Winds* was afflicted with a subtle duplicity
that compromised the "facts" of Gloucester's and the
world's reality. *Four Winds* lacked

> the will to be as fine as
>   as fine as fins are
>   as firm as
>   as firm as mackerel is
>   (fresh out of water)
>   as sure
> as sure as no owner is
(M, 20)

Ferrini, in other words, was the literary counterpart of the
absentee-owner. His editorial instincts were not *of*
Gloucester; they patronized the eclectic and precious cultural fashions that characterized, in Olson's opinion, the
typical "literary" quarterly. " . . . you / are more like
Gloucester now is / than I who hark back to an older polis"
(*M*, 20), he chided.

The notion of "polis" is the moral center of gravity of
The Maximus Poems. "Polis" is a nucleus of true believers,
an ideal, an obedience, an integrity and a prime of value.
But also,

> polis is
> eyes
(M, 26)

The select few of each civilization who make up "polis"
can be identified by the care and attention they pay to limits ("Limits / are what any of us / are inside of" [*M*, 17]).

Moulton's jibe to the "green-horn," "'Where'd you get those glasses?'" calls his attention to his violation of those limits:

> I'd picked three swordfish out of the sun-blaze
> where no regular could afford to look,
> to waste his eyes seeking a fin in that place
> > (*M*, 26)

For fishermen and for poets the lesson is the same: "polis" demands

> the attention, and
> the care
> > however much each of us
> > chooses our own
> > kind and
> > concentration
> > > (*M*, 28)

As the repository of civilization's attention and care, "polis" is unquestionably elite:

> so few
> have the polis
> in their eye . . .
> So few need to,
> to make the many
> share (to have it,
> too)
> > (*M*, 28, 29)

And yet, what could be more secularly egalitarian than its simple government:

> There are no hierarchies, no infinite, no such many as
> > mass, there are only
> eyes in all heads,
> to be looked out of
> > (*M*, 29)

One notable member of "polis," Marsden Hartley, is

celebrated in "Letter 7." Hartley, the American artist and poet who painted the Gloucester landscape in 1931, is the centerpiece for a gallery of "polis" types. Since "polis is / eyes," it is Hartley's eyes and those of his local painter friend, Helen Stein (*M*, 18), which set the theme. The quality of their vision is linked to "that carpenter's" (*M*, 30), William Stevens, a shipbuilder who came to Gloucester in 1642 and proved his commitment to his own inner obedience by speaking out against royal interference and consequently losing his freedom. Stevens's "polis" status is assured by Olson's speculation that he "must have been the first to see the tansy / take root" (*M*, 30). A few lines later Maximus goes so far as to muse, "I think he was the first Maximus" (*M*, 31). Something of the nature of "polis" is suggested by the assertion that Stevens "was the first to make things, / not just live off nature" (*M*, 31). One of his specific "traits," which sets him apart, is presented in this stammering utterance: "necessities the practice of the self,/ that matter, that wood" (*M*, 31). The syntax and punctuation may be eccentric, but the meaning springs right out of Olson's definition of "objectism" in "Projective Verse": "a word to be taken to stand for the kind of relation of man to experience which a poet might state as the necessity of a line or a work to be as wood is, to be as clean as wood is as it issues from the hand of nature, to be shaped as wood can be when a man has had his hand to it" (*HU*, 59). Stevens, Hartley, and Stein all share, it would seem, an integrity of craft that the vision of "polis" affords them.

Perhaps the phrase "the practice of the self" prompted Olson to define the quality of "polis" craftsmanship more precisely, for he proceeds to catalogue a number of artistic eccentricities—"cracks" in the wood (*M*, 31, 32)—which "polis" nevertheless tolerates. He alludes to Verrocchio (whose name, incidentally, means "true eye"), Pound, and two Gloucester denizens, Al Gorman and Mason Andrews, as example of

> How much the cracks matter, or seams in a ship, the
>   absolutes
> of swelling (the mother), of weather (as even in

                    machine parts,
          tolerance
                         (*M*, 32)

Even though the standards of "polis" allow "millimeters"
of "'play'" in "the exactness [of the] caulking" (*M*, 32), they
permit "no latitude, any more than any, elite" (*M*, 32). The
eccentricities that result from one's personal obedience,
yes; "carelessnesses," no. Olson even includes an example
of his own "carelessness" to help make the point:

          "Why did you give him a black hat,
          and a brim?" she queried,
          "when he wore tennis shoes,
          and held his pants up
          with a rope?"
                              (*M*, 31)

The remark is Olson's first wife, Con's, and she refers to
Maximus's earlier allusion to Pound:

          . . . the great man, in his black coat and wide hat, the
                         whole man
          wagging, the swag
          of Pound
                                        (*M*, 28)

Con has picked up a "carelessness" in her husband's inaccurate description (his "arrogations") of Pound which, it
appears, he admits to, but defends on the grounds of other
older and more legitimate eccentricities that "polis" certainly sanctioned:

          (as he used to wear a turquoise
          in one ear, London,
          to let them know, here
          was an American savage)
                              (*M*, 32)

   Hartley, of course, demonstrated similar eccentricities
that were the consequences of his "practice of the self" (*M*,

31). The more sensational of these closes the "letter":
"Hartley's hands . . . were so much (each finger) their own
lives' acts . . . refusing women's flesh" (*M*, 34). Homosex-
uality represented no bar to "polis," nor did deviance from
Olson's personal principles of craft. Hartley, for example,
attempted and achieved "transubstantiations" (*M*, 33) of
rocks into cloth, gulls into palms, monoliths into apostles,
which were the kind of symbolic allegorizations that Olson's poetics anathematized:

> Such transubstantions
> > as I am not permitted
> > nor my father,
> > who'd never have turned the Whale Jaw back
> > to such humanness neither he nor I, as workers,
> > are infatuated with
>
> > > (*M*, 33)

The "practice of one's self," therefore, falls well within
those "millimeters" of tolerance "polis" allows. Indeed,

> The men of this city
> (who was it did carve the lady?)
> are never
> doctrinaires
>
> > (*M*, 34)

In *The Special View of History* Olson confessed, "I do go in
circles, in fact believe that only if one does does one finally
suck up the vertu in anything" (*SVH*, 35). His method in
Maximus, of course, is the same. The epic rarely proceeds
in straight lines but rather moves in spirals, picking up
subjects and themes again and again, each time from a
somewhat different approach. The parallel concerns of
"Letter 3" and "Tyrian Businesses" is a case in point. The
"tansy city, root city" that is addressed in "Letter 3" is not
the comprehensive group of citizens that the ancient
Maximus of Tyre actually addressed, for "Polis now /
is few" (*M*, 11), not, as it was in the Tyrian's time, all. Thus,
Maximus's present address is to

Only a man or a girl who hear a word
and that word meant to mean not a single thing the
least
   more than
what it does mean (not at all to sell any one anything,
   to keep them
                 anywhere . . .
                       (*M*, 11)

The semantics of "polis" are absolute; they admit no duplicity. They eschew the invidious excesses of "mu-sick"
that seek to "sell" and enslave. They provide an appropriate vocabulary for "Root person in root place" (*M*, 12). It is
this kind of ancient integrity in language and act that the
morning "exercise" (*M*, 35) in "Letter 8" seeks to attain
once again. The model for such integrity is, of course, the
dance, because its content and form are identical ("who
can tell the dancer from the dance"). Since he wishes to
transpose the integrity of dance to the act of writing, Olson
proposes the "exercise" as:

how to dance
sitting down
   (*M*, 35)

The movement of this exercise is a disciplined one back
to "root" words. It is a search for etymon:

There may be no more names than there are objects
There can be no more verbs than there are actions
                       (*M*, 36)

Where such a search for etymons takes place, of course, is
the dictionary, and the essence of "Tyrian Businesses" is
indeed just that—a dictionary exercise. Webster's co-
authors the heart of this "letter," providing, in fact, definitions (which Olson cites verbatim) for "heart," "ling,"
"nasturtium," "tropic bird," "futtock," and "fylfot." The
most thematically significant definition, however, is for
"metacenter":

(When M is above G, all's
well. When below, there's
upset. When M and G are coincident
it is not very interesting)

(*M*, 36)

Further use of Webster's definition of "metacenter" appears in part 5 of the "letter";

Ukase: "the vertical
              through the center of buoyancy of a
floating body
              intersects
the vertical through the new
center made....

(*M*, 38)

Established as a "Ukase," "metacenter" suggests a recommended stance for maintaining the kind of center of gravity that dance or any buoyant act of craft requires. In fact, another definition, that of "felicity," is posed as the goal of all craft in such a way that the ukase, metacenter, is implied as "felicity's" mode:

"felicity
resulting from life of activity in accordance with"
Which is the question: in accordance with what?
Ukase: "the vertical..."

(*M*, 38)

As it was his custom to do in *Call Me Ishmael*, Olson related "felicity" and "metacenter" with a "fact": Moulton's folly. Because the Captain of the ship "Hawes" violated "felicity" by perverting the use of his vessel for greed ("Moulton had been that greedy, he wanted to pick up all the lumber we see floating ahead of us on the sea.... For the garage he was building, Rockport" [*M*, 38]), he lost the proper "center of gravity" for his ship and its crew. The crew grew careless ("... it was party stuff—even the cook had gone below, he was so bored" [*M*, 39]), and, with pat-

ent irony, it turns out to be the "metacenter" of the buoyant floating lumber that repays Moulton's greed:

> What happened was, Moulton fetched the vessel
> straight on one plank plunk in its middle, and
> it stayed there, right in its center, even when
> it swayed below water . . . never losing . . .
> the center of her Moulton had hit her by.
> <div align="right">(<i>M</i>, 39)</div>

The lumber, floating on the water in the shape of a "fylfot," "scarfed together to form . . . futtocks" (*M*, 40),
maintained a "life of activity in accordance with" the ukase
of "metacenter"; it was Moulton and the "Hawes" that did
not and who consequently suffered from the "fylfot . . .
who calls herself / (luck" (*M*, 40).

Assuring felicity by maintaining a proper metacenter is
perhaps no more than a variation on Olson's old familiar
theme that one should possess a proper "stance towards
reality." Here, however, the "stance" is elucidated in terms
of integrity; it is a posture that brooks no division of intention and act, form and content, means and end. It is the
kind of oneness that Olson discovers in "Letter 9" in the
plum and similar "things / which don't carry their end any
further than / their reality in / themselves" (*M*, 42). Such
"self-things" (*M*, 43) as the plum and the book (*In Cold Hell,
In Thicket*), to which he compares it, draw his admiration
because their "likeness is to nature's, / not these tempestu-
ous / events" (*M*, 43). The book, in particular, is a "self-
thing" because it is one of "the tasks

> I obey to,
> not to a nation's,
> or at all to history
> or to a building. . . ."
> <div align="right">(<i>M</i>, 43)</div>

The primary concern of *The Maximus Poems* up to this
point has been to establish the nature of "polis," the ideal
society, in contrast to "pejorocracy," a debased materialistic world. "Letter 10" begins the historical reach of the

poem by probing the beginnings of these values in Gloucester. It concerns "founding: was it puritanism, / or was it fish?" (*M*, 45), but characteristically absorbs that historical issue into the present[13]:

> And how, now, to found, with the sacred & the
> profane—
> both of them—
> wore out
>
> (*M*, 45)

What Olson is interested to demonstrate, as L. S. Dembo points out, is the "general triumph of Puritanism over the more 'authentic' values,"[14] which, of course, are the true "metacenter" of Gloucester's essence—fish:

> It was fishing was first. Only after (Naumkeag)
> [Salem]
> was it the other thing
>
> (*M*, 45)

Roger Conant's house, in fact, was "snatched to Salem" (*M*, 46) by Governor Endecott, an act that models the victory of the puritan "smug of Salem" (*M*, 47) over fish. Endecott is designated by Olson as "the first of, / the shrinkers" (*M*, 46) who through Puritan principles "shrank" the Elizabethan expansiveness of the fish economy and even Conant's "Tudor" house. A modern Conant, James Bryant, president of Harvard, is inversely condemned as a "dilater" of puritan money on the basis that "Harvard / owns too much" (*M*, 47). Thus, even the potential "polis" of Harvard is "destroyed" (*M*, 47) by Conant and the "pejorocratic" beginnings of the nation are assured by Endecott. Only Gloucester itself keeps its metacenter, remains "polis":

> As you did not go,
> Gloucester: you tipped, you were our
> scales
>
> (*M*, 46)

In his verse "Obit" for Black Mountain College, Olson wrote

> The last man of the place
> dreamed
> of 14 persons on this hillside
> like the mountain in the Chinese classic
> to whom all those repaired who were useless,
> the empire had become that good it was impossible
> it was so dull, . . .[15]

The "14 persons" are a "polis" that originally established their presence in Gloucester in the "Stage Fight" that sets the moral historical center of gravity for *The Maximus Poems*. The fight occurred about 1626 and involved fourteen Dorchester fishermen, who took over a fishing "stage" that the Puritans had never got around to using [" . . . hadn't yet got to / fishing that season (stayed in bed)" (*M*, 112)]. Hewes, the leader of the fishermen, was forced to give way when Miles Standish and his Puritans finally arrived. Olson's sympathies in the matter are clear:

> They should raise a monument
> to a fisherman crouched down
> behind a hogshead, protecting
> his dried fish
>
> > (*M*, 114)

These fourteen were "polis" because, like the "Lady of good voyage," they were obediently true to the "facts" of reality. They knew that in the New World

> Venus
> does not arise from
> these waters. Fish
> do
> > (*M*, 58)

They were obedient to the "elements men stand in the midst of" (*M*, 6) and, as Dembo points out, they were "'artisans' rather than exploiters."[16] Like their successors at

Black Mountain, they were heroic failures before adversaries that refused in this new land "to do it anew" (*M*, 45). Thus, the "Stage Fight" represents, like Endecott's "snatching" of Conant's house, a victory of Puritanism over the commercial integrity of early Gloucester. In Olson's mind the moral for Gloucester perhaps fit Black Mountain, too:

>   the newness
>   the first men knew was almost
>   from the start dirtied
>   by second comers
>
>   (*M*, 135)

The "second comers" failed to see, as John White, the founder of the Dorchester fishing settlement on Cape Ann in 1623, "had seen it / in his eye" (*M*, 108), the *real* Gloucester. "Polis is / eyes" (*M*, 26), but Miles Standish and his puritan "Moses men" could not see "the things / of this world (New / world" because of their need "to twist" them "back to Covenantal / truth)" (*M*, 130). Even Covenantal truth, however, was no guard against the pressures of material plenty:

>   Wow sd Pilgrimes ONE HALF MILLION BUCKS in
>   5 years from
>   FURS at the same time FISH . . .
>
>   (*M*, 109)

Not commerce itself but the manner in which commerce is conducted was the issue. The heroic Dorchester "14," Olson would have us believe, were motivated by "the adventure / of the new frontier / (not boom, or gold, / the lucky strike, / but work" (*M*, 104). A natural integrity informed their endeavors that was absent from the exploitive mercantilism of the puritans who drove them off the fishing stage. Olson's point here and throughout *Maximus* is clear: "Because of the agora America is, was, from the start, the moral struggle" (*M*, 62).

Olson's pantheon of heroes in this moral struggle, his "polis," includes, of course, John White and Roger Con-

ant, but most of his admiration is reserved for Christopher
Levett and John Smith. Although Levett never set foot on
Cape Ann (he was an early settler on the coast of Maine),
Olson saw "polis" in him because he possessed the "care /
to be right" and could "pay attention, / to what fishermen /
(since when? before / 1500) have / been showing: the motion / (the Westward motion) / comes here, / to land" (*M*,
121), "Care," "attention," and the knowledge that "It wasn't
new, / what happened, / at Cape Ann. It's where, / and
when it / did" (*M*, 121) won Olson's esteem of Levett. This
man, he felt, understood that the "Westward motion" of
the New World settlements was precisely what he had described to Herbert Kenny: "the final movement of the
earth's people, the great migratory thing."

　　Indeed, as Maximus notes, "Levett is a measure" (*M*,
133). He speaks "of what he's done

> ("I have obtained a place
> of habitation in New-
> England, where I have built
> a house, and fortified it
> in a reasonable good fashion,
> strong enough against such enemies
> as are those Savage people")
> 　　　　　　　　　(*M*, 134)

Conant and Levett put down their "two houses / by fish
flakes and stages / on rocks near water with trees / against
sea" (*M*, 134). They chose to live where they worked,
maintaining an appropriate balance between man's need
and nature's plenty. They were the antithesis of "absentee
ownership," but soon—almost immediately—pejorocracy,
the "dirtiness of goodness" (*M*, 134), would corrupt that
noble beginning. "We know," Maximus ruefully observes
from the advantage of today,

> what Levett Smith or Conant
> didn't, that no one
> knew better
> than to cash in on it.
> 　　　　　(*M*, 135)

Captain John Smith was just as unpejorocratic as Levett, and Olson employs him as an effective contrast to the puritanism of Miles Standish:

> The Capteyne
> he was, the eye he had
> for what New England offered,
> what are other than
> theocratic, why we are
> not at all what the Mediterraneans
> think we are
>
> (*M*, 50)

Olson identified Smith as a "Sea-Marke" (*M*, 69, 122), the title of a poem Smith himself composed, which is a wrecked ship that serves as a warning to other ships of shoals:

> "Aloofe, aloofe; and come no neare,
>   the dangers doe appeare;
> Which if my ruine had not beene
>
>   you had not seene:
> I onely lie upon this shelfe
>   to be a marke to all
>   which on the same might fall,
> That none may perish but my selfe . . ."
>
> (*M*, 69)

This "sea-marke," Smith, is also "the stater of / quantity and / precision . . . who knew private / passivity," but it is his enigmatic association with the "princes / of the husting" and the "terrible / inert of / nature (the Divine Inert . . ." (*M*, 122) that is his most puzzling feature. Olson's essay "Equal, That Is, to the Real Itself" provides a helpful gloss. In attempting to elucidate Melville's ability to present "the actual character and structure of the real itself," Olson writes:

> I pick up on calm, or passivity, Melville's words, . . . He says somewhere a harpoon can only be thrown accurately from such repose as he also likened the White

> Whale to, . . . a mighty mildness of repose in swiftness is
> his phrase. Likewise, in handling Ahab's monomania, he
> sets up a different sort of a possible man, one of a com-
> pany which he calls the hustings of the Divine Inert.
> (HU, 122)

Olson wanted to stress the powerful energy that lay dis-
guised in the apparent "rest" of the "inertial structure of
the world" (HU, 122) and was convinced that Ahab's
monomania was a "husting"—a bit of political campaign-
ing—for this "terrible / inert of / nature" (M, 122). In
Maximus, he would add Smith too to that group of exemp-
lars of the real, making the point that although Smith appears to be an unusually passive agent of "polis" ("Smith
also got shoved aside" [M, 49]), "Smith / changed / everything . . ." (M, 124).

The evocations of John Smith, Miles Standish, the Stage
Fight, the early tensions between "Covenantal" and "fishing" interests collaborate in a value system that seems to
justify Maximus's ubiquitous discoveries of "polis" and
"pejorocracy" in his "sea city." Dembo's opinion that "the
Maximus Poems are unified by a specific reading of the history of Gloucester and Cape Ann" that "aims at the revelation of moral truth"[17] is certainly sound in regard to those
"letters" that are grounded in "a specific reading of the
history," but what of those "letters" that, with lyrical intimacy, address themselves to private experiences and even
personal dreams? One entire sequence beginning with
"The Twist" and ending with "Letter 22," for example, is a
deliberate interruption of the historical context into which
it is thrust. It is even cordoned off, so to speak, from the
"COLD-SOCIAL"[18] tone of the material that precedes and
follows by the significant words "la vérité" (M, 81) and
"The facts" (M, 99). It is as if a nonfactual, imaginative
interlude were being formally announced.

"The Twist," with its wealth of connotation in the title,
opens the theme of the sequence that can be summarized
perhaps as the changes in the adornment in which honor is
clothed. Specifically, "Twist" means "nose-twist," or the

nasturtium. Maximus had earlier specified this flower as "my beloved, my / trophy" (*M*, 36). In "Maximus, at Tyre and Boston," he reaffirms that commitment: "the nasturtium / is my shield" (*M*, 93). Since the sequence works largely in dream material, the nasturtium, as Maximus's flowery escutcheon, parallels the function of the shield given to Aeneas by Vulcan in Virgil's epic; both shields are worked with prophetic visions of future events and heroes of Rome and, presumably, Gloucester (prophetic for Gloucester in the sense that it is "future" in relation to the historical content into which it has been placed). But "twist" also retains the meaning of a change in direction or orientation that rather neatly sets up at least one strategy of the sequence—to register whatever changes in the "moral truth" of Gloucester might be evident from a contemporary perspective.

Indeed, the fact that the poem that precedes "The Twist," "On first Looking through Juan de la Cosa's Eyes," involves a more or less "original" first experience of "The New Land" (*M*, 78) would make it seem, as Sherman Paul observes, that it is a companion poem to "The Twist,"[19] for "The Twist," too, opens with Olson's journey and first experience of a "New Land"—Gloucester. Thus, we are prepared to experience whatever "twists" might separate the first impressions of Juan de la Cosa and Olson/Maximus.

A sense of that historical déja vu is conveyed by the way Maximus employs the antique language of Captain John Smith to characterize his present-day "discovery" of "the country not discovera" (*M*, 85). What he specifically discovers (emblematically in this case) are the "dog-rocks / the tide roars over" and how the tide

> shoots
> calyx and corolla by the dog
> (August,
> the flowers break off
> but the anther,
> the filament of now, the mass
> drives on

> (*M*, 85)

The "dog-rocks" are Gloucester's Scylla and the flowers ("the nasturtium / is my shield") are escutcheons, visible blazons of honor, which in the roaring of the tide lose their adornments (their *"honor," "color," "point,"* in the technical vocabulary of blazonry) but retain "the anther, / the filament of now." Honor, in other words, changes its outward fashions as "the mass drives on," but nevertheless maintains a constant integrity that is assured by the "anther." This anther, in fact, is what so grasps Olson's admiration:

>   the whole of it
>   coming,
>   to this pin-point
>   to turn
>   in this day's
>   sun
>   (*M*, 85)

The essence of honor, underlying its traditional signs, is also evoked by "my daughter, naked / on the porch" (*M*, 88). She, like the anther of the flower, holds the potential "splendor" (*M*, 94) of whatever outward show of honor "now" requires. In fact, a primary intention of the sequence is "to make it ['The real'] / clear (to clothe honor / anew" (*M*, 92). Honor's clothing changes but its essence remains constant—the calyx and the corolla break off, but the anther stays. This point seems to inform the allusion to Newman Shea in Letter 20. Shea, we are told, "had stolen a crew's pay / 30 or 40 years before / The story / you could never get straight, / it was only, as always" (*M*, 91). Shea's actual crime is unremembered, but the bar on his escutcheon lives. Olson concludes that

>   it is not the substance of a man's fault,
>   it is the shape of it
>   is what lives with him, is what shows
>   in his eyes (in our eyes
>
>   (*M*, 91)

A man's virtues and faults—his honor—emerge from a

quality that "shows / in his eyes"—in the flower's instrument of potentiality, the anther. In a word, "Polis is eyes"
and reveals itself not in antique clothes, but in the latest
fashion of "now."

A "duel" in a Marine Corps training camp documents
another instance in which "twists" in honor's outward
fashion have failed to affect its naked essence. After con-
ceding that the traditional vocabulary of honor ("Tree of
Battles," "palette fess nombril base") is mere "yack-yack"
and "Professor stuff," Maximus notes how Red Hanna and
Red Rice once tried each other's trust "at 20 paces, / M-12's
/ at a hundred yards / to stand to it, to see / if though they
blanched they'd hold, / they'd chance / the other's / error"
(*M*, 89). The test of honor is unquestionably at stake in the
duel, even though the form is bizarrely modern. One is
tempted to assume that this "duel" was the occasion "five
years ago, when she [honor] lost / her last stitch / of
clothes" (*M*, 89), for what that confrontation proved was
that despite the language and form used to justify the
duel, the "anther" of honor—its "shape" and its "eyes"—
remained constant, only awaiting the occasion to be
"clothed . . . anew" (*M*, 92).

Honor, then, is essentially timeless and is a quality that
adapts itself to the season much like a flower. It is even the
kind of flexible firmness—aim rather than anchor—that
gives *Maximus* a formal integrity:

> And if the nasturtium
> is my shield
> > and my song
> a cantus firmus
> > > (*M*, 93)

Most of all, however, honor is the hallmark of "polis":

> we who throw down hierarchy,
> who say the history of weeds
> is a history of man,
>
> do not fail to keep

> a sort of company: all
> is how the splendor is worn
>   (*M*, 94)

In the pejorocratic present the splendor is obviously not worn well. "The world of the Hannas / (the world of Earp) / went with the blueberries" (*M*, 92), but its disappearance needs no "crying over." Instead, we should rise to the challenge "to clothe honor/ anew" and to make certain that when "the heat's on, / when it's your dice or mine, all / or nothing, that she be there / in all her splendor" (*M*, 92).

If a "specific reading of the history of Gloucester and Cape Ann" unifies the *Maximus Poems* by providing "the revelation of moral truth," as Dembo claims, the word *history* must be appreciated in its Herodotean sense as verb (*'istorin*) rather than noun, as "finding out for one's self" rather than relying on second-hand report, as the past-alive-in-the present rather than dead chronology. After all, the premise of Maximus's Gloucester is that it is time-less—not "a city" but "City," the "fillet of the rose . . . the fire of the energy patterns." As the "image of creation and of human life for the rest of the life of the species," Gloucester is a repository and source of history itself. Thus, the "splendor" of honor is as retrievable in a dice game as in the fields before the gates of Troy, in the tidal roar of the Annisquam river as in any Homeric Scylla and Charybdis. To gather up the "energy patterns" of history into moral truth requires a poet adept at the art of *'istorin*, one who understands his own life as an allegory (*SVH*, 28) and evokes the moral truth of "history" through the evidence of his own experiences. Thus, the imaginative, personal sequences of *Maximus*, such as the one just considered, at the very least complement the "COLD-SOCIAL" history of the other letters and testify to Olson's Herodotean conviction

> that we are only
> as we find out we are
>   (*M*, 95)

NOTES

1. The phrase is Roy Harvey Pearce's. See *The Continuity of American Poetry* (Princeton, N.J.: Princeton University Press, 1961), p. 83. I accept Pearce's broad sense of the term *epic* and apply it freely to American long poem equivalents.
2. William Carlos Williams, *Paterson* (Norfolk, Conn.: New Directions, 1963), p. 2.
3. Ibid., p. 53.
4. See Ed Dorn, "What I See in *The Maximus Poems*," in *The Poetics of the New American Poetry*, ed. Donald Allen and Warren Tallman (New York: Grove Press, 1973), pp. 293–307.
5. William Carlos Williams, "The Fatal Blunder," *Quarterly Review of Literature* 2 (1944): 126.
6. See Marjorie Perloff, "Charles Olson and the 'Inferior Predecessors': 'Projective Verse' Revisited," *ELH* 40 (Summer 1973): 285–306. Perloff's intention is to demonstrate that Olson's poetics are almost totally derivative of Pound and Williams, but her point extends by implication to the poetry as well.
7. Letter to Henry Well, Apr. 12, 1950, *The Selected Letters of William Carlos Williams*, ed. John C. Thirwall (New York: McDowell, Oblensky, 1957), p. 268.
8. Olson, "'I know men for whom everything matters': Charles Olson in conversation with Herbert A. Kenny," *Olson* 1 (Spring 1974): 9.
9. Ibid., pp. 19–20. Olson elaborates further by alluding to Vilhjalmur Stefansson's *The Northward Course of Empire* (New York: Harcourt, Brace, 1922): "Or take Stefansson . . . that the motion of man upon the earth has a line, an oblique, northwest-tending line, and Gloucester was the last shore in that sense. The face that the continent and the series of such development as have followed, have occupied three hundred and some-odd years, doesn't take away that primacy or originatory nature that I'm speaking of. I think it's a very important fact. And I of course use it as a bridge to Venice and back from Venice to Tyre, because of the departure from the old static land mass of man which was the ice, cave, Pleistocene man and early agricultural man, until he got moving, until he got towns. So that the last polis or city *is* Gloucester" (p. 20).
10. Olson, "On 'History,'" *Olson* 4 (Fall, 1975): 43.
11. Ibid., p. 44. These words are actually Robert Duncan's, who is attempting to clarify a previous remark by Olson to Allen Ginsberg during a discussion at the University of British Columbia, Vancouver, 29 July 1963.
12. Ibid.
13. Olson makes pointed allusion to Mircea Eliade's *The Sacred and the Profane* (New York: Harcourt Brace, 1959), which attempts to isolate and describe two dimensions of human experience: the irra-

tional (sacred) and the natural (profane). Presumably Olson sees both dimensions devitalized in modern pejorocratic times.

14. L. S. Dembo, "Charles Olson and the Moral History of Cape Ann," *Criticism* 14 (Spring 1972): 167.

15. Olson, "Obit," *Olson* 2 (Fall 1974): 59.

16. "Charles Olson and the Moral History of Cape Ann," p. 166.

17. Ibid., p. 165.

18. In striving for "a music as complex as reality is," Olson felt a poet should make the music "COLD (in order that no Swindler-Charlatan—Orator ever get in. . . . It's going to be tough. That is, how am I going to *increase* (intensify) such as the K[ingfisher]s (is not the MAXIES essentially of the same order, with my person as adolescent and child allowed in, to relieve that COLD-SOCIAL (????". From unpublished Notes, "Continuation of thoughts carried over from Notebook I" (CtU), quoted in Robert von Hallberg, *The Scholar's Art* (Cambridge, Mass. and London: Harvard Univ. Press, 1978), p. 192.

19. Sherman Paul, *Olson's Push* (Baton Rouge, La., and London: Louisiana State University Press, 1978), p. 156.

The Mode of the Mythologist:
Maximus IV, V, VI and Beyond

> What I am about to say will seem, I'm
> sure, frightfully abstract if you don't
> see that I am making pictures––that I
> am what I am interested in: a
> mythologist.
> —*The Special View of History*

Eight years separate the publication of *The Maximus Poems* (1960) and *Maximus IV, V, VI* (1968) and although the continuity of the epic seems formally maintained (some of the poems of *Maximus IV, V, VI* are conscious reconsiderations of specific "letters" in *The Maximus Poems*), one can sense a difference. George Butterick, for instance, is struck with "how the range opens up" from the previous volume. "There is an effort to drive back to roots," he notes, "both of Gloucester as the end of migrating Western man, and of man himself, back to the deglaciation and the sources of civilization."[1] Robert von Hallberg is impressed by Olson's "greater freedom with his materials," specifically evident in his willingness to compromise with "historical accuracy." He charges that Olson "flirts with what he knew to be specious history" and that he falls back for coherence upon the very "EGO-POSITION" he had condemned in Pound's *Cantos*.[2] Sherman Paul sees Maximus making the "new start" he had announced in "Letter, May 2, 1959" (*M*, 150). He feels that the new start was necessary because "history has brought him to an impasse and for the time being exhausted his historiographic impulse."[3]

Whether the "difference" in *Maximus IV, V, VI* is mere reaction to a methodological impasse, a stepped-up level of a form inchoately evident in the preceding volume, or the floundering of a poet-in-decline who has lost his way is a moot issue. Sympathetic readers might insist that whatever historical impasse Maximus may have experienced was not really so much an impasse but an inevitable progression from the mode of *'istorin* to the more sweeping range of myth that an epic form might be expected to exhibit. They might point to the slight shift in locus—from the City of Gloucester to Dogtown—as an obvious instance of the poet seeking a suitable arena for a cosmos of archetypes ("go inland, to / Dogtown: the Harbor / the shore the City / are now / shitty" [*M2*, 7]). As for any alleged deepening of the obscurity of the sequence, they surely would argue that Olson, like Homer and Hesiod, was using "a wholly different syntax . . . in which the words and actions reported are set down side by side in order of their occurrence in nature, instead of by an order of discourse, or 'grammar,' as we have called it" (*AP*, 52).

Detractors, on the other hand, might tend to view the "new start" as self-indulgent decline, the confused, eccentric mutterings of an Olson who has lost direction as well as ballast. After all, *The Maximus Poems* were written largely at a time when Olson was at the peak of his energies and from the stabilizing comfort of a private "polis," Black Mountain. *Maximus IV, V, VI*, by contrast, was composed by a relatively rootless performer who capitalized on (and was corrupted by) the uncritical adulation of student audiences during the sixties and who lost the "care" and "attention" that saved the obscurities of his earlier work.[4]

For good or for bad, *Maximus IV, V, VI is* different. It *is* a "new start," not in methodology or essential form but in range and ambition. In *The Maximus Poems* the quest was a local one and the vision was inward: "the thing you're after / may lie around the bend" (*M*, 1); "in! in! the bowsprit, bird, the beak / in, the bend is in" (*M*, 4). The "lady of good voyage" was *poised* for epic "forwarding" (*M*, 2), but she never really left Gloucester Harbor. Her weights and materials were essentially there; she was New England. In *Maximus IV, V, VI*, however, the anchor is hoisted,

Gloucester, as an historical reality, recedes, and the reader confronts an open, unpaginated sea inhabited by almost unlimited primordial serpents and beasts and mythical heroes and deities. At the very least, Olson is explicitly "getting rid of nomination" (*ML*, 26); his vision has magnified; his poem gropes for size.

The fact is that Gloucester, even though geographically and culturally the "final migratory act of man," is from another point of view merely a new point of departure in Maximus's quest. The "last polis or city *is* Gloucester," Olson conceded, but "man is either going to rediscover the earth or is going to leave it."[5] The "new start" that Maximus chooses is obviously the rediscovery of the earth, and this entails a reverse journey, a retracing of that migratory, "oblique, northwest tending line" that marks the "motion of man upon the earth." Toward this end Maximus makes a vow:

> that forever the geography
> which leans in
> on me I compell [*sic*]
> backwards I compell Gloucester
> to yield, to
> change
>   Polis
> is this
>
>   (*M2*, 15)

One of the most forceful changes Maximus exerts on Gloucester is size. *Maximus IV, V, VI* is an exercise in mythic magnification. "I take it myths are only large pictures of pictures, enlargements," Olson said. "A reenactment, as Malinowski learned from the Trobriands, does enlarge in that it celebrates what men have selected from what their ancestors did which seemed to them useful" (*SVH*, 57). Because Gloucester itself has finally succumbed ("as the Nation ... the World" [*M2*, 7]) to modern corrupton, Maximus leads us inland to the stony wastes of Dogtown. The creatures with whom he populates Dogtown's morraine are mythically enlarged into archetypal figures of Hittite,

Egyptian, Norse, Algonquin, and Greek imaginations. The tale of the "Handsome Sailor" Merry (*M2*, 2–6) sets the pattern. The local tale of a man driven by drunken pride to disprove an alleged flagging of his bullfighting prowess is provided a mythically furnished context drawn from Hesiod, Heraclitus, and particularly Erich Neumann.[6] As a consequence, Merry himself is magnified to mythic status and becomes the first in a series of epic giants whose cosmic struggles—*enantiodromia* (*SVH*, 57–58)–are documented by Maximus. The methodology of magnification, Olson wants it clearly understood, is no mere literary trope; it is a cultural imperative:

> This, is no bare incoming
> of novel abstract form, this
>
> is no welter or the forms
> of those events, this,
>
> Greeks, is the stopping
> of the battle
>
> 　　　　It is the imposing
> of all those antecedent predecessions, the precessions
>
> of me, the generation of those facts
> which are my words, it is coming
>
> from all that I no longer am, yet am,
> the slow westward motion of
>
> more than I am
>
> 　　　　　　　　　　　　　　　(*M2*, 14)

The literary "imposing of . . . antecedent predecessions" is Maximus's attempt to restore and consolidate that sense of man's potential size that the Greek mind had reduced and limited. Through the act of myth Maximus hopes to evoke "all that I no longer am, yet am." Myth will gather up in a collective community the whole of "westward" migrating man, and so it is wrong to assume that Maximus's enterprise is mere "novel abstract form." It is much more ambitious. It is a "stopping of the battle" that the Greeks waged and continue to wage against the realization of man's original size. It is Maximus marshalling those "precessions" of himself into a voice greater than his own.

If this is a "new start" resulting from a historical or formal impasse encountered in the original *Maximus Poems*, it would be hard to prove it from Olson's past assertions. The stress and intensity of the commitment may be stronger in *Maximus IV, V, VI*, but the ideas had been discussed endlessly before, at least as early as "The Gate and the Center":

> (We are only just beginning to gauge the backward of literature, breaking through the notion that Greece began it, to the writings farther back ... When I say gauge, I am thinking that we have *no* measure of what men are capable of, . . . But just because of our own late, & Western, impression we continue to shy, in our present disgust with such muscularity, away from all such apparent magnifications as epic and myths seem to include. (*HU*, 20)

Maximus himself is, of course, the ultimate epic, mythic "magnification" to whom the other heroes of the entire *Maximus* sequence are related. Butterick describes a note Olson wrote in which he relates not only the "Handsome Sailor" Merry to Maximus, but other "archetypal figures" as well: Orion, Hercules, Gilgamesh, Samson, Odysseus, Theseus, etc. These are described as "'Bigmans types' or 'Sons,' with their monstrous opponents (such as Merry's bull) 'the libido hung up on MA'—specifically, the Terrible Mother of Jungian interpretation." The note reports that "outside such" heroes and monsters as these "stands 'Maximus Anthropos' as 'the MODEL of man without this STRIFE.' He has numerous other names and guises throughout the poems—shipwright William Stevens, the androgynous John Smith, Enyalion, the Perfect Child,

Odysseus, Hercules Melkaart, James Merry, Manes/Minos, even a 'whelping mother,'"[7]

What magnification achieves is the celebration of man and a "*human* universe"—not man as he is thought to be, but man as he can be and once was. Thus the mythic "gods" that Maximus includes among the archetypal figures of Dogtown are no grander than men; they are rather models of aboriginal humanity. Olson is unabashedly euhemeristic on this point: "gods are men first . . . and how many generations does it take to turn a hero into a god?" (*HU*, 17). Thus, the epic quest is naturally drawn back to the beginnings of man, before the Greeks achieved his humiliation:

> I have this dream, that just as we now cannot see & say the size of these early HUMAN KINGS, we cannot, by the very lost token of their science, see what size man can be once more capable of. (*HU*, 21)

Myth is the vehicle of magnification, but "we long ago lost the POINT & PURPOSE of what we call—and thus kill—the act of myth" (*HU*, 21).

We killed myth by formalizing it into dead fiction instead of vital act. Myth ought to be (and presumably is intended to be in *Maximus*) what Olson endorsed as its best definition: "the spoken correlative of the acted rite, the thing done" (*SVH*, 21). This definition asserts the *performative* rather than the declarative function of myth. Ideally, myth does not merely tell us things but *does* things to us. It is a verbal "doing"—a participatory act—which, by repeating the "doings" of anterior cultures, effects that transhistorical consolidation of mankind that brings meaning to such assertions as "the slow westward motion of / more than I am." Indeed, the ritual of myth enlivens man's awareness that he is "more than" just himself. All history and all cultures come together in the immediate present through the reenactment of the mythic rite. Myth shares with history, poetry and religion, Olson insisted, "the common property that a thing done is not simply

done but is re-done or pre-done. It is at once com-
memorative, magical, and prospective" (*SVH*, 22).

The mythic magnifications of *Maximus IV, V, VI* strive for
this performative ideal. Formally, of course, they can also
be appreciated as Olson's "correction" of Pound and Williams by "getting rid of nomination, so the historical material is free for forms now" (*ML*, 26), but so much of the
material in these later sequences goes beyond the merely
historical, and even the patently historical items are imbued with mythic transcendence. What really distinguishes
Maximus IV, V, VI as a "new start" is the way it intensifies
the earlier method of *'istorin* (itself a penultimate mythic
mode) into mythic act itself. The intensification is pro-
found and arresting, for it marks Olson's beginning of a
complete commitment, epistemologically and aesthetically,
to the principles of a truly "Human Universe," It is a
reorientation of basic assumptions and attitudes so comprehensive that it deserves the label *religious*.

Religious is a perilous word to use in connection with a
Maximus who has declared, "I have known the face / of
God. / And turned away, / turned, / as He did, / his
backside" (*M*, 88), not to mention an Olson who is proud to
have devised both a cosmology and a mythology "*without
letting God in*" (*SVH*, 55). But one can perhaps make a distinction between formal theistic belief and a religious "attitude" oriented to something beyond one's conscious ego,
even something as vaguely defined as Olson's "something
we are in the hands of" or "the life in us."[8] At the very least
a religious attitude informs one's obedient passivity to the
"slow westward motion of / more than I am" (*M2*, 14).

The collective, primordial esprit de corps that characterizes Olson's object of obedience gives away his in-
debtedness to Carl Jung. In Jung's "Collective Unconscious"
Olson found the suitable "deity" for his alternative world—
his "Human Universe." While it was unquestionably
"human," the Collective Unconscious also possessed
the requisite religious attribute of "otherness." "While the
contents of the personal unconscious are felt as belonging
to one's own psyche," Jung explained, "the contents of the

collective unconscious seem alien, as if they come from outside."[9] The Collective Unconscious also provided an inner equivalent of Creation—an inner cosmos as infinite as the cosmos outside of us—which served as the psychic equivalent of outer empirical terrain. In fact, Olson once defined "mythology" as "the kosmos inside a human being" (*SVH*, 53). Its impact on Olson carried to the very act of perception itself. Echoing Merleau-Ponty, Olson insisted that the object perceived is "the motive not the cause of the event."[10] In a radically "human" universe, all so-called "causes" must, by definition, be "motives," that is, all events must be humanly initiated. Jung substantiates this position absolutely:

> Everything that is unconscious in man is projected by him into an object situated outside his ego, so that the phenomenon of projection is a part of the natural life of the psyche, a part of human nature itself.[11]

The Unconscious, in other words, "projects" attributes into objects and those attributes accordingly lure the perceiver's attention. The act of perception, therefore—the "knowledge-bring event," to use Merleau-Ponty's term—is not *caused* by an inert object. Rather it is the perceiver who "causes" (motivates) the act by virtue of his having in fact imbued the object with an attention-lure to start the whole process. This reversal of the traditional assumptions about perception naturally pleased Olson because it lent epistemological support for the "human universe" that he persistently championed, but he also saw its advantage for the writer. "The narrative that gets started begins to be the story that will yield from the object a *raison* that causes us in the first place to give our attention to it," he explained. "And it is therefore . . . 'the motive and not the cause of the event.' Which is very exciting, to get the whole thing reversed, so that we don't have cause anymore, we have motive. And again we inherited a complete system of discourse for two thousand years which has absolutely crapped motive. . . . So that the tendency of the objective world to go away from us has been extremely strong."[12]

Thus, Olson blames our fall from a "human universe" to a "universe of discourse" on our willingness to allow "motive" to be supplanted by "cause." The point is fundamental; it is a key that unlocks many of the obscurities in Olson's position, for what is the distinction between "chronicle" and the "his-story" that results from *'istorin*, or, for that matter, the distinction between history and myth, if it is not the fact that one is governed by cause and the other motive? Our motivational grasp upon the universe is what Olson's work consistently strives to restore, even though his tactics to achieve that restoration have not always remained precisely the same.

When he wrote "The Human Universe," for example, Olson asked, "Can one restate man in any way to repossess him of his dynamic?" (*HU*, 8). "Systematic particulars" was the only suggestion he had then, but in *Maximus IV, V, VI his* thinking on the problem had progressed to myth. Since myth is an act that is "re-done or pre-done"—a reenactment of ancient rites—it is the repository of not only the personal motives of an author but of the primordial motives of all men from all time. Through myth one finds access to the archetypes that make up the Collective Unconscious and thus gains the potency, size, and power that that primordial matrix offers. Through myth the shallowness and perversity of our collective modern psyche—the pejorocracy of our contemporary times—can find remedy, its psychic anemia dispelled by an inrushing of primordial blood. Thus, in *Maximus IV, V, VI* Olson gives us a liturgy of archetypal events that hold within them root human motives. Because they are the motives of collective mankind, they "speak" to the most diverse people and appear to have an almost magical attraction.

In this sense perhaps we can see how Olson's incessant search for "that with which we are most familiar" is not very much different from Jung's similar quest for primordial awareness through the process of "individuation." In both cases the goal is that which is collectively familiar and which therefore quickens the collective motives of those who experience it through myths. Here is an example of a poem in *Maximus IV, V, VI* that overtly strives to tap the power inherent in the primordial images it employs. It serves as a fairly reasonable model for the mythic mode characterizing the other poems of the volume:

> I forced the calm grey waters, I wanted her
> to come to the surface I had fought her,
> long enough, below. I shaped her out of
> the watery mass
>
> and the dragger, cleaning its fish,
> idled into
> the scene, slipped across the empty water
> where I had placed
> the serpent, staring as hard as
> I could (to make the snow
> turn back to snow, the autos
> to come to their
> actual size, to stop
> being smaller,
> and far away. The sea does
> contain the beauty I had looked at
> until the sweat
> stood out in my eyes. The wonder is
> limitless, of my own term, the compound
> to compound until the beast rises from the sea.
>   (*M2*, 32)

If the word were not anathema to Olson, one might be tempted to call this poem an allegory. It hums the resonances that are generated by the words *water*, *sea*, *serpent*, and *beast*. It touches the fairy tales we have been told, the sagas we have experienced, the epics we have read, but it also evokes even deeper recollections that go beyond our conscious memories. Thus, we are tempted to assign allegorical meanings to the serpent, to the water, to the sea, in order, perhaps, to gain a control over these feelings that the poem arouses in us. All this happens even without Jung's helpful suggestions that in even the oldest traditions the serpent was regarded "as the personification of the destructive as well as the life-giving power of water," and that he also "symbolizes the state of primordial unconsciousness, for this animal likes to haunt 'caverns and tenebrous places,'" or even that "Tiamat, the dragon symbolizing the darkness of the beginning, is often represented as a 'raging serpent,' who is conquered by Marduk, the sun hero."[13] The simple act of struggle the poem "does" (re-does?) for us is a struggle we seem innately to know, for it emerges from a shared archetypal matrix.

To be sure, we can easily find allegorical "meaning" in the passage. Perhaps Maximus struggles to dredge his unconscious to the conscious surface of his awareness as the final act of an individuating process. In less overtly Jungian terms, perhaps the act represents the artist struggling to "land" the objet d'art that he "shaped . . . out of the watery mass." But the point of mythic presentation is not allegory (that would be referential to the "doing" of the rite rather than the "doing" itself) but participation by responding directly to the primordial images as they have an impact upon ourselves. Presumably, Olson created (chose?) the event for the powerful archetypal response it evoked in him without any further regard to what possible impact it might have upon another. Thus, the "open-endedness" of the mythic mode that, like the religious parable, is "drawn from nature or common life" but arrests the hearer "by its vividness or strangeness . . . leaving the mind in sufficient doubt about its precise application to tease it into active thought."[14]

A more complicated illustration of the mythic mode is the "Maximus, From Dogtown" poems, "I" and "II." The saga of James Merry is obviously "loaded" with powerful primordial images. Besides the prominent archetypal motif of Merry's struggle with the demonic beast, there is the controlling image of the "WATERED ROCK" that initially sanctifies the pasture meadow where Merry meets his Dogtown demise, but which later mythically organizes a welter of apparently dissimilar archetypes into what for Olson, at least, was an apparently satisfying primordial experience. Jung helps us trace the archetypal impulses by pointing out that the Moon, as mistress of moisture, was the "mother of 'Hydrolith,' the water-stone—another name for the *lapis* and hence for Christ."[15] Elsewhere he notes that Saint Ambrose "says the water from the rock is a prefiguration of the blood that flowed from Christ," and that "another alchemical text mentions the 'water from the rock' as the equivalent of the universal solvent, the *aqua permanens*."[16] It may well be, as Butterick suggests, that "WATERED ROCK" simply refers to "the geological condition of Dogtown,"[17] but Olson's capitalization of the term and the fact that it becomes a recurrent motif throughout "Maximus, From Dogtown—I" and "II," suggest that he felt some integrating power in the notions of Christ's blood and *aqua permanens*.

Some of that integrating power can be seen in how water proves to be the solvent that eats an access to the "Age / *under* / Dogtown" that appears to be the final destination of the poem's mythic journey:

> the greater the water you add
> the greater the decomposition
> so long as the agent is protein
> (*M2*, 10)

Thus, the water image, introduced in the saga of Merry, gathers intensity in the second "Dogtown" poem by serving as a kind of cultural solvent that penetrates through geological time to the "Carboniferous / Pennsylvania" period of the Paleozoic era. Olson's familiar backward "advance" is literal as well as figurative here, delving geologically from "earth" through "ice" and "stone" eventually to "Carbon." But it is a spiritual return as well. The solvent also carries with it the association of Christ's blood, and as we journey back to "Aquarian Time," the obvious association of "fish" in turn draws a second association with "Christ" ("Christ o Christ pick the seeds / out of yr teeth—how handsome / the dead dog lies!"). "Handsome" links Christ with Merry (the "Handsome Sailor"), but it is probable that the "seeds" in Christ's teeth were similarly intended to link Christ (and thus Merry too) to the "Black Gold Flower." We may surmise this from the intriguing association Jung makes in this significant phrase: "the seeding-place of the diamond body in the golden flower."[18] The word *diamond*, of course, also makes its appearance in the poem ("the 'mother' / rock: the Diamond" [*M2*, 10]). What these associations seem to imply is that the geological, cultural, and spiritual journey backwards and down through time and earth seeks a matrix ("Migma") from which such primordial figures as Merry and Christ (in this poem) and "He-with-the-House-on-his-Head" (*M2*, 7, 31), "she-who-Lusted After-the / Snake-in-the-Pond (*M2*, 7, 21–22) (in later legendary tales), not to mention Maximus himself, emerge. This matrix exists deep in "the *under* / vault" where "carbon, mother-rock," and diamonds harbor the "Throne of Creation" that turns out to be also the "Black Gold Flower." The poem takes us to a Source—the source of geological history, but more important the source of man's primordial energy and wisdom: the Collective Unconscious.

Jung would characterize this journey as "individuation," the process whereby the conscious ego is confronted with the hidden power of the unconscious, resulting in a sense of wholeness characterized by the word *Self*. Olson's poem has a similar therapeutic thrust, although the "Self" he strives to effect is no individual blend of the conscious and unconscious, but an individuation of civilization itself: in short, a salutary reintegration of the "Universe of Discourse" with the "Human Universe."

Since "Maximus, From Dogtown—II" specifically reduces the various figures of wholeness to a primal symbol of Self—the mandala of the "Black Gold Flower"—that mandala deserves special attention. According to Jung, the mandala signifies "nothing less than a psychic centre of the personality not to be identified with the ego," and upon first seeing the text of Richard Wilhelm's translation *The Secret of the Golden Flower*, he was prompted to write himself on the subject of the mandala.[19] In his commentary to that book, he identifies the "secret" as "the light of

Heaven ... the Tao,"[20] and delivers an account of one man's contact with the light:

> Once well started on my quest, I found myself traversing a succession of spheres or belts ... the impression produced being that of mounting a vast ladder stretching from the circumference towards the center of a system, which was at once my own system, the solar system, and the universal system, the three systems being at once diverse and identical.... Presently, by a supreme effort... I succeeded in polarizing the whole of the convergent rays of my consciousness into the desired focus. And at the same instant ... I found myself confronted with a glory of unspeakable whiteness and brightness.[21]

Maximus alludes to a strikingly similar "ladder" and integrating experience:

> up Dogtown hill on top one day the
> Vertical American thing will
> show from heaven the Ladder
> come down to the Earth
> of Us All, the many who
> know
>   there is One!

The two ladders both lead to a "center of a system" that, in Olson's poem, turns out to be, predictably,

> Polis, the Child-Made-Man-Woman is
> (Mary's Son
> Elizabeth's
> Man) MONOGENE
>   (M2, 9–10)

"Mary's Son" does double duty as a reference to Olson's own "self" (his mother's name was Mary) and, again, as yet another Christ allusion. Similarly, "Elizabeth's man" turns on the fact that his second wife's name was Elizabeth, with the secondary suggestion of the "Elizabethan" or Renaissance man. Of key significance here, however, is the curious word "MONOGENE," which Olson picked up from Jung's *Psychology and Alchemy*. There, during a discussion of "how the center of the circle [the psyche] which expresses . . . a totality would correspond not to the ego but to the self as the summation of the total personality," he quotes a Gnostic example from the treatise of the Codex Brucianus:

> This same is he [Monogenes] who dwelleth in the Monad, which is in the Setheus, and which came from the place of which none can say where it is . . . . This same is the Mother-City . . . of the Only-begotten . . . . By way of explanation I should add that "Setheus" is a name for God, meaning "creator." The Monogenes is the Son of God.[22]

Monogenes, a denizen of the "Mother-City" and "Son of God," is Olson's natural image of Self, but a Self that includes not only Olson, but all of "polis" too. The integrated nature of "MONOGENE" is suggested by the fact that he is "Child-Made-Man-Woman," that is, he is Jung's *animus* and *anima* in healthy balance.

Olson is no Christian, and his exuberant employment of Christ figures throughout the *Maximus* poems might mislead readers if they do not understand that in all the primordial figures he invokes in his epic he is merely trying to present pictures of the integrated Self, the "total personality" not yet split by discourse. Those familiar with his prose know how often he refers to Jung's expression that "the self is not only the centre, but also the whole circumference which embraces both conscious and unconscious; it is the center of this totality, just as the ego is the center of consciousness."[23] Olson's own Maximus is of course an obvious archetype of the self, but so is Christ, Merry, Stevens, Tartaros, Typhon, and all the other archetypal heroes of *Maximus*. The Self, as Jung saw the archetype and as Olson employs it, parallels God and also stands for the life-process. It is symbolized, as Jung points out, by the circle, square, quaternity and the mandala, all features, incidentally, of the "Black Gold Flower."

The nature of Maximus takes on considerable light when he is considered as an archetype of Self, for we can then see that he is not merely Olson's *conscious* awareness but that he includes as well the circumference bounding the conscious and *un*conscious of not only Charles Olson but the collective archetypes of all mankind. It is in these later *Maximus* poems that Maximus probes the mythic regions at the circumference of the Self. Thus, although the philosophy of Whitehead holds privileged status in Olson's thought, *Maximus IV, V, VI* and *The Maximus Poems: Volume Three* are dominated by the rhythms and modalities of the Jungian vision. Not that there exists a conflict in Olson's mind between Whitehead and Jung. To the contrary, Whitehead's "three stages of feeling" (*SVH*, 50) neatly parallel Jung's stages of individuation. In both cases (a point not lost on Olson) the goal was to effect a cultural reintegration through which the ego-ridden, pejorocratic insulation of contemporary civilization might be broken by the fertile energies available to it from its hidden psychic half, the Collective Unconscious. That hidden half resided on the other side of Greece, ultimately in Sumer, and access to it finally could be nothing less than myth.

Jung once said, "I do not regard the symbol as an allegory or a sign, but take it in its proper sense as the best possible way of describing and formulating an object that is not completely knowable."[24] The definition is probably broad enough to evade Olson's objection that symbols are referential to reality rather than of it. In fact, few would care to argue that one of the primary strategies discernible in the *Maximus* poems is just such an employment of the Jungian "symbol." Take *fish* as one prominent example. Even though fish is the major industry of Gloucester and, as Olson would argue, the original economic base of the New World, Maximus regards it as a visible measure of the unknowable essence of his city. To be an authentic artisan, for example, one must be as "fine as fins are / ... as a mackerel is" (*M*, 20). In Gloucester "fishing was first" and

the city's promise lay in its possession of "fins / for forwarding" (*M*, 45). Fishing is pitted against Puritanism, as if
both were figures in some kind of cosmic morality play, the
sacred and the profane reduced to a "symbolic" struggle
over the rights to a fishing stage. As far as Maximus is concerned, fishermen are almost automatically granted
"polis" status unless they adulterate the purity of their
calling through greed or "inattention," as Moulton did.

In these later *Maximus* poems, Olson's symbolic fish res-
onate with archetypal significance but without losing any
of their "particularism." Olson felt confident to exploit the
resident, primordial "magic" of such words as *fish*, *stone*,
water, fully assured that their latent energies would be automatically released by his mythic mode. One example is a
poem inspired by Robert Duncan's spontaneous realization (conveyed in a letter to Olson) that "Maximus . . . [was]
a magic opus—not as magical or imagination but as a rec-
ipe that had to be followed."[25] Appropriately, the poem
was entitled, "for Robt Duncan / who understands / what's
going on" (*M2*, 37–39).

Fish is the literal and the symbolic core of the poem. It
appears initially as a "particular" that arouses disgust ("the
pile of rotting fish—fish!"), but soon matures into one of
those Jungian "shadows" that the conscious ego must confront before it proceeds to individuation ("as my life 'rot-
ted' . . . my mother . . . 'spoiling' / me"), and finally, as a
vehicle for social criticism ("fish sticks, pictures / will be
necessary on the covers of the TV dinners / to let children
know that mackerel is a different / looking thing than herrings"). *Fish* works quite well as a cohesive element in the
poem, but, as Duncan perhaps sensed, a kind of "magic"
inheres in the word—a primordial resonance—that Olson
was cleverly able to coax from it. The vehicle for his gentle
coaxing is the tiny phrase "decline of fishes."

The phrase occurs within a context of pejorocratic disgust. Maximus has just dismissed his idyllic catalogue of
"Dogtown's people" as "romantic / stuff I promised never
to leave life riding on," and begins a series of ancient-
modern contrasts that are clearly moral judgments:

"mutos" is held in contrast to "Pegasus"; "nature" is compared to "the inhumanity of Nazi crematoria ("furnaces men shoot / bodies into"); "man" is measured against the anemic abstraction "species"; and finally, "love" is juxtaposed to self-love ("for ourselves alone"). At this point, Maximus tries to defend the "romantic" procedure he was lured into before by explaining:

> I walk you paths of lives I'd share with
> you simply to make evident the world
> is an eternal event and this epoch solely
> the decline of fishes

He intends, of course, to continue his list of moral contrasts; this time pitting the "eternal event" (the world) against "the decline of fishes." Obviously this is no careless mixing of economic and metaphysical interests. The "decline of fishes" carries far more evocative power than the falling off of an industry, far more than the physical putrefaction of fins, scale, and flesh; it mightily stands as a cosmological symbol evoking the disparity of the contemporary pejorocracy with the "eternal" standard of the world's event. And most importantly it does this *without* our conscious awareness of the cultural significance of *fish*: that it is a fundamental Christian symbol, and that it serves not only as the "bridge between the historical Christ and the psychic nature of man," but as "a psychological concept of human wholeness."[26] These are Jung's words, but the point both he and Olson share about symbols such as *fish* is that people *instinctively* respond to suggestions such as the "decline of fishes" as models depicting some sort of fall from human wholeness. Thus, the "decline of fishes" means the decline of "polis." The power already resident in the primordial word need only be gently nudged into archetypal vibrations that wrench an otherwise undistinguished poem into powerful suggestiveness.

Maximus IV, V, VI and *The Maximus Poems: Volume Three* strive for this effect. They harness archetypal images with little deliberate purpose other than the release of power

that results. The released power itself is assumed sufficiently adequate to "make evident the world / is an eternal
event." What authorial control that remains is nothing
more than Olson's confidence that he has kept himself
creatively obedient to the integrating call of his Self from
whence the images come.

Jung had a name for this kind of creative strategy. He
called it the "visionary" mode that he contrasted to its
counterpart, the "psychological."[27] The "psychological"
mode draws for its material on the "realm of human consciousness," from the "vivid foreground of life." Accordingly, the "psychological" writer is "directed and purpose-
ful." In his view, "his material is only material, and entirely
subject to his artistic purpose; he wills to present this and
nothing else." "Visionary" art, on the other hand, treats
what Jung describes as a

> strange something that derives its existence from the
> hinterland of man's mind—that suggests the abyss of
> time separating us from pre-human ages, or evokes a
> superhuman world of contrasting light and darkness. It
> is a primordial experience which surpasses man's un-
> derstanding, . . . It arises from the timeless depths; it is
> foreign and cold, many-sided, demonic and grotesque.

The method of the visionary artist is predictably passive.

> works positively impose themselves upon the author; his
> hand, as it were, seized, and his pen writes things that
> his mind perceives with amazement. The work brings
> with it its own form . . . . [The writer's] consciousness
> stands disconcerted and empty before the phenomenon
> [and] he is overwhelmed with a flood of thoughts and
> images which it was never his aim to beget . . . Yet in
> spite of himself he is forced to recognize that in all of
> this his self is speaking, . . . he can only obey and follow
> the apparently foreign impulse.

Discounting some of the florid tone of Jung's description of the "visionary" mode, we can see its striking simi-

larity to Olson's "projective" stance. The writer "obeys" some force beyond his consciousness, for example, and yet that force is acknowledged to be the Self. Similarly, form is determined (extended) by content and not imposed by the conscious will of the author. Finally, the literary product is not a work shaped by the conscious aim of its creator, but the material is permitted to retain much or all of what Jung calls its original "refractory obstinacy."

But is it enough merely to label Olson a "visionary"? Even as a "visionary" poet has he really penetrated much beyond the "EGO-POSITION"? Are not his readers at the mercy of his eccentric obedience, captive to the "centre and the circumference" of his Self? Olson's defense is at the ready. His is not an "EGO-POSITION." for the Self he obeys is not "EGO"; it is a dependable object of obedience and devotion that is, from his Jungian perspective, decidedly "other." Since that Self is "other"—rooted in the Collective Unconscious—it is common with all other humans and so his obedience to it can hardly be called eccentric.

A great deal is left to faith—faith in the "Special View" of history, faith in a "human Universe," faith in Olson himself. To appreciate the poetry requires buying the whole package, that we convert, as it were, to Olson's "stance towards reality." Other poets, of course, have asked this of their readers. Yeats, for example, was a committed proselytizer for beliefs many would consider silly, but his poetry was powerful enough to render his silliness irrelevant. Can the same be said of Olson? Is his poetry *as poetry* sufficiently strong to balance the gnomic obscurities of such pages as these:

> Aristotle & Augustine
> clearly misunderstood Anaximander
> And in so doing beta'd
> themselves
>
> (*M2*, 113)

or,

>   *tesserae*
>   Commissure
>   (*M2*, 99)

or,

>   In the harbor
>   Can 9 Nun 8
>   Nun 10 Can 11
>   (*M2*, 132)

Granted, we have Butterick's exhaustive *A Guide to the Maximus Poems of Charles Olson* to help us puzzle out the lay of Olson's mental terrain as he wrote these "poems," but the scholar's joy in forcing such refractory obstinacies to light must be measured against the sympathetic reader's frustration and bewilderment. "I've never decided," confesses Samuel Charters, with refreshing candor.

> whether or not Olson considers his poems difficult to follow, or if he cares, but he is difficult, . . . Sometimes . . . it's because he doesn't give enough away—at other times . . . because he includes a maze of only distantly related material. Probably, since he knows the inference of everything he's saying he doesn't see the difficulty at all. And even if he does see it the work is interrelated, and he could have decided that if he's opaque at one point the same reference will come up again at a point where the light hits a little more strongly.[28]

The power and charm of Charter's apology for Olson resides in his patient, trusting capitulation to the poetry—his willingness to obey its energies and acts rather than its meanings (clarification is always just around the bend). His practical advice on the hermeneutical problems Olson's verse raises, even couched as it is in bewildered desperation, is helpful and sound, but this advice was intended for *The Maximus Poems* and the earlier poetry. What would he *advise for Maximus IV, V, VI* and *The Maximus Poems: Volume Three*?

Perhaps he might fall back on one of Olson's literary heroes, D. H. Lawrence, and unabashedly concede that conciliation with Olson's poetry is nothing less than a moral act. "The essential function of art," said Lawrence,

> is moral. Not aesthetic, not decorative, not pastime and recreation. But moral . . . a passionate, implicit morality which changes the blood, rather than the mind. Changes the blood first. The mind follows later.[29]

Olson's poetry *does* strive to "change the blood" and, with it, the heart, the mind, and the physiology. His poems are performative moral acts that demand as much allegiance to the rigid doctrines that support them as any orthodox religion. But is this a poetry that will have lasting and enriching impact upon generations to come? An honest guess would be no. Olson's verse is so captive to doctrine, so overwhelmed by the larger "push" of his extra-literary "positions," that it has no independent life of its own. The engines that drive it hum in the pages of Olson's theoretical prose, and, exciting and promising as that theory may be to other poets, it only occasionally finds vindication in Olson's own verse. Too much of the cranky arbitrariness of the maverick philosopher, the anthropologist, the historian, the philologist, and the mythologist intrudes upon the verse for it to evade completely the charge of propaganda. It reveals itself finally as an instrument of a higher cause that rarely has time for its own concerns. On brief occasions when it does—those instances that critics invariably trot out as examples of the kind of lyric talent Olson can exploit when he wants to—we are charmed by an authentic "lyrical interference of the individual as ego" that, alas, Olson (as doctrinaire theorist) is obliged to damn. No, the Maximus in Olson could never be content merely to create poems. He was always after more . . . so much more.

NOTES

1. George Butterick, *A Guide to the Maximus Poems of Charles Olson* (Berkeley, Calif.: University of California Press, 1978), p. xl.

2. Robert von Hallberg, *Charles Olson: The Scholar's Art* (Cambridge, Mass., and London: Harvard University Press, 1978), pp. 110-11.

3. Sherman Paul, *Olson's Push* (Baton Rouge, La.: Louisiana State University Press, 1978), p. 181.

4. See Hugh Kenner, *A Homemade World: The American Modernist Writers* (New York: Alfred A. Knopf, 1975), p. 182.

5. Olson, "I know men for whom everything matters," *Olson* 1 (Spring 1974): 20.

6. Erich Neumann, *The Great Mother: An Analysis of the Archetype*, trans. Ralph Manheim, Bollingen Series, vol. 47 (New York: Pantheon Books, 1955), pp. 221-22.

7. Butterick, *Guide*, p. xxix.

8. Unpublished lecture, "To Make It Clear" (CtU).

9. Carl Jung, *Collected Works*, trans. R.F.C. Hull, 2d ed., Bollingen Series 20 (Princeton, N.J.: Princeton University Press, 1968), 8: 312.

10. *Olson* 3 (Spring 1975): 48.

11. Jung, *Collected Works*, 9:87.

12. *Olson* 3 (Spring 1975): 48.

13. See Jolande Jacobi, *Complex/Archetype/Symbol*, trans. Ralph Manheim, Bollingen Series, vol. 57 (Princeton, N.J.: Princeton University Press, 1959), p. 146.

14. C. H. Dodd, *The Parables of the Kingdom*, rev. ed. (New York: Scribner's, 1961), p. 16.

15. Jung, *Collected Works*, 12: 388.

16. Ibid., 9: 87-88.

17. Butterick, *Guide*, p. 242.

18. Jung, *Collected Works*, 12: 104n.

19. Ibid., 12: 95.

20. *The Secret of the Golden Flower*, trans. Richard Wilhelm, rev. ed. (New York: Harcourt, Brace & World, 1962), p. 101.

21. Ibid., p. 105.

22. Jung, *Collected Works*, 12: 102-4.

23. Ibid., 12: 41.

24. Ibid., 9: 73.

25. Butterick, *Guide*, p. 246.

26. Jung, *Collected Works*, 9: 182-83.

27. See Morris Philipson, *Outline of a Jungian Aesthetics* (Evanston, Ill.: Northwestern University Press, 1963), pp. 106-11.

28. Samuel Charters, *Some Poems/Poets* (Berkeley, Calif.: Oyez, 1971), p. 27.

29. D. H. Lawrence, *Selected Essays* (London: Penguin, 1950), p. 28.

Selected Bibliography

Writings of Charles Olson

Additional Prose: A Bibliography on America, Proprioception, & Other Notes and Essays. Edited by George F. Butterick. Bolinas, Calif.: Four Seasons Foundation, 1974.

Archaeologist of Morning. New York: Grossman Publishers, 1973.

A Bibliography on America for Ed Dorn. San Francisco: Four Seasons Foundation, 1964.

Call Me Ishmael. New York: Reynal and Hitchcock, 1947.

Causal Mythology. Edited by Donald Allen. San Francisco: Four Seasons Foundation, 1969.

Charles Olson: Reading at Berkeley. Transcribed by Zoe Brown. San Francisco: Coyote, 1966.

"Definitions by Undoings." *Boundary 2* 2 (1973–74): 7–12.

The Distances. New York: Grove Press, 1960.

Human Universe and Other Essays. 1965. Reprint. Edited by Donald Allen. New York: Grove Press, 1967.

"'I know men for whom everything matters': Charles Olson in conversation with Herbert A. Kenny." *Olson* 1 (1974): 7–44.

In Adullam's Lair. Edited by George F. Butterick. Provincetown, Mass.: To the Lighthouse Press, 1975.

In Cold Hell, In Thicket. Palma de Mallorca: Divers Press, 1953.

"Introductory Statement for Black Mountain College Catalogue, Spring Semester, 1952." *Olson* 2 (1974): 25–27.

"Journal of Swordfishing Cruise on the Doris M. Hawes." *Olson* 7 (1977): 3–42.

"Language Is a Thumb." Unpublished manuscript. Literary Archives of the University of Connecticut Library.

"Lear and Moby Dick." *Twice A Year* 1 (1938): 165–89.

Letters for Origin, 1950–1955. Edited by Albert G. Glover. London and New York: Cape Goliard Press/Grossman Publishers, 1970.

The Maximus Poems. New York: Jargon/Corinth Press, 1960.

The Maximus Poems/1–10. Stuttgart: Jonathan Williams, 1953.

The Maximus Poems/11–22. Stuttgart: Jonathan Williams, 1956.

Maximus Poems IV, V, VI. London and New York: Cape Goliard Press/Grossman Publishers, 1968.

The Maximus Poems: Volume Three. Edited by Charles Boer and George F. Butterick. New York: Grossman Publishers, 1975.

Mayan Letters. Edited by Robert Creeley. London: Grossman Publishers/Cape Editions, 1968.

"A New Short Ars Poetica . . ." Unpublished manuscript. Literary Archives of the University of Connecticut Library.

"Notes for the Proposition: Man Is Prospective." *Boundary 2* 2 (1973–74): 1–4.

"Obit." *Olson* 2 (1974): 59–64.

"On 'History.'" *Olson* 4 (1975): 40–46.

Pleistocene Man: A Curriculum for the Study of the Soul. Buffalo, N.Y.: Institute of Further Studies, 1968.

Poetry and Truth: The Beloit Lectures and Poems. Edited by George F. Butterick. San Francisco: Four Seasons Foundation, 1971.

The Post Office. Edited by George F. Butterick. Bolinas, Calif.: Grey Fox Press, 1975.

"Pun as True Meaning as Well as of Rhyme." Unpublished manuscript. Literary Archives of the University of Connecticut Library.

"The Secret of the Black Chrysanthemum." *Olson* 3 (1975): 64–92.

Selected Writings of Charles Olson. Edited by Robert Creeley. New York: New Directions, 1967.

Spearmint & Rosemary. Berkeley, Calif.: Five Trees Press, 1975.

The Special View of History. Edited by Ann Charters. Berkeley, Calif.: Oyez, 1970.

Stocking Cap. San Francisco: Four Seasons Foundation, 1966.

"There Are Four Measurements . . ." Unpublished manuscript. Literary Archives of the University of Connecticut Library.

"To Make It Clear." Unpublished manuscript. Literary Archives of the University of Connecticut Library.

"Under the Mushroom: The Gratwick Highlands Tape." *Olson* 3 (1975): 3–57.

Other Sources

Adams, Brooks. "Charles Olson and the Vatic." *Boundary 2* 2 (1973–74): 26–37.

———. *The Law of Civilization and Decay: An Essay on History.* New York: Knopf, 1948.

———. *The New Empire.* New York: Macmillan Co., 1902.

Aiken, William. "Charles Olson: A Preface." *Massachusetts Review* 12 (1971): 57–68.

Allen, Donald M., ed. *The New American Poetry: 1945–1960.* New York: Grove Press, 1960.

Allen, Donald M., and Creeley, Robert, eds. *New American Story.* New York: Grove Press, 1965.

Allen, Donald M., and Tallman, Warren, eds. *The Poetics of the New American Poetry.* New York: Grove Press, 1973.

Apsel, Maxine. "The Praises." *Boundary 2* 2 (1973–74): 263–68.

Babbitt, Frank Cole. "The E at Delphi." In *Plutarch's Moralia.* Vol. 5. The Loeb Classical Library. 14 vols. Cambridge, Mass.: Harvard University Press, 1936.

Bertholf, Robert. "Righting the Balance: Olson's *The Distances.*" *Boundary 2* 2 (1973–74): 229–49.

Bly, Robert. "A Wrong Turning in American Poetry." *Choice* 3 (1963): 33–47.

Boer, Charles. *Charles Olson in Connecticut.* Chicago: Swallow Press, 1975.

Butterick, George F. *A Guide to the Maximus Poems of Charles Olson.* Berkeley, Los Angeles, London: University of California Press, 1978.

Butterick, George F., and Glover, Albert G., eds. *A Bibliography of Works by Charles Olson.* New York: Phoenix Book Shop, 1967.

Byrd, Don. *Charles Olson's Maximus.* Urbana, Ill.: University of Illinois Press, 1980.

Charters, Ann. *Olson/Melville: A Study in Affinity.* Berkeley, Calif.: Oyez, 1968.

Charters, Samuel. *Some Poems/Poets.* Berkeley, Calif.: Oyez, 1971.

Christensen, Paul. *Charles Olson: Call Him Ishmael.* Austin, Tex.: University of Texas Press, 1975.

Combs, Maxine. "Charles Olson's 'The Kingfishers': A Consideration of Meaning and Method." *Far Point* 4 (1970): 66–76.

Corman, Cid, ed. *The Gist of Origin.* New York: Grossman Publishers, 1975.

Corrigan, Matthew. "Materials for a Nexus." *Boundary 2* 2 (1973–74): 201–28.

Creeley, Robert, ed. *Mayan Letters.* London: Jonathan Cape, 1968.

—————, ed. *Selected Writings of Charles Olson.* New York: New Directions, 1966.

—————. "Some Notes on Olson's *Maximus.*" In *Yugen 8.* New York: Totem Press, 1962, pp. 51–55.

Dahlberg, Edward. *The Confessions of Edward Dahlberg.* New York: George Braziller, 1971.

Davenport, Guy. "Scholia and Conjectures for Olson's 'The Kingfishers.'" *Boundary 2* 2 (1973–74): 250–62.

Davey, Frank. "Poetry and Truth: The Beloit Lectures and Poems." *Boundary 2* 2 (1973–74): 24–25.

—————. "Six Readings of Olson's *Maximus.*" *Boundary 2* 2 (1973–74): 291–322.

Dawson, Fielding. *The Black Mountain Book.* New York: Croton Press, 1970.

—————. "A Letter from Black Mountain." *Olson* 2 (1974): 4–7.

Dembo, L. S. "Charles Olson and the Moral History of Capre Ann." *Criticism* 14 (1972): 165–74.

—————. *Conceptions of Reality in Modern American Poetry.* Berkeley, Calif.: University of California Press, 1966.

—————. "Olson's *Maximus* and the Way to Knowledge." *Boundary 2* 2 (1973–74): 279–90.

Dickey, James. *Babel to Byzantium: Poets & Poetry Now.* New York: Farrar, Straus and Giroux, 1968.

Dorn, Edward. "What I See in *The Maximum Poems.*" In *The Poetics of the New American Poetry*, edited by Donald Allen and Warren Tallman, pp. 293–307. New York: Grove Press, 1973.

Duberman, Martin. *Black Mountain: An Exploration in Community.* New York: E. P. Dutton, 1972.

Duncan, Robert. "From a Notebook." *Black Mountain Review* 5 (1955): 209–12.

—————. "Notes on Poetics: Regarding Olson's *Maximus.*" *Black Mountain Review* 6 (1956): 201–11.

Eliade, Mircea. *The Sacred and the Profane.* New York: Harcourt Brace and Co., 1959.

Fenollosa, Ernest. *The Chinese Written Character as a Medium for Poetry.* Edited by Ezra Pound. San Francisco: City Lights Books, 1936.

Flegg, H. Graham. *From Geometry to Topology.* London: The English Universities Press Ltd., 1974.

Ford, O. J. "Charles Olson & Carl Sauer: Towards a Methodology of Knowing." *Boundary 2* 2 (1973–74): 145–150.

Fuller, Roy. *Owls and Artificers.* London: Andre Deutsch, 1971.

Ginsberg, Allen. *Allen Verbatim.* Edited by Gordon Ball. New York: McGraw-Hill Book Co., 1974.

Glover, Albert G., ed. *Letters for Origin.* New York: Cape Goliard Press/Grossman Publishers, 1970.

Gunn, Thom. "New Books in Review." *The Yale Review* 50 (1961): 585–96.

Harrison, Jane. *Ancient Art and Ritual.* London: Thornton Butterworth, Ltd., 1913.

Ingber, Richard G. "Number, Image, Sortilege: A Short Analysis of 'The Moon Is the Number 18.'" *Boundary 2* 2 (1973–74): 269–72.

Jacobi, Jolande. *Complex/Archetype/Symbol.* Translated by Ralph Manheim. Bollingen Series, vol. 57. Princeton, N.J.: Princeton University Press, 1959.

Jung, Carl. "Commentary." In *The Secret of the Golden Flower.* Translated by Richard Wilhelm, pp. 81–137. Rev. ed. New York: Harcourt, Brace & World, Inc., 1962.

———. *The Integration of the Personality.* Translated by Stanley Dell. New York: Farrar and Rinehart, 1939.

———. *Symbols of Transformation. Collected Works of C. G. Jung.* Translated by R. F. C. Hull. Vol. 15. Bollingen Series 20. Princeton, N.J.: Princeton University Press, 1970.

Kenner, Hugh. *A Homemade World: The American Modernist Writers.* New York: Alfred A. Knopf, 1975.

Lawrence, D. H. *Selected Essays.* London: Penguin, 1950.

Lieberman, Marsha, and Lieberman, Philip. "Olson's Projective Verse and the Use of Breath Control as a Structural Element." *Language and Style* 5 (1972): 287–98.

Matthiessen, F. O. *American Renaissance: Art and Expression in the Age of Emerson and Whitman.* New York: Oxford University Press, 1941.

Merleau-Ponty, Maurice. *Signs.* Translated by Richard C. McCleary. Evanston, Ill.: Northwestern University Press, 1964.

Neumann, Erich. *The Great Mother: An Analysis of the Archetype.*

Translated by Ralph Manheim. Bollingen Series 47. New York: Pantheon Books, 1955.

Ossman, David. *The Sullen Art: Interviews with Modern American Poets.* New York: Corinth Books, 1963.

Paul, Sherman. *Olson's Push: Origin, Black Mountain and Recent American Poetry.* Baton Rouge, La.: Louisiana State University Press, 1978.

Pearce, Roy Harvey. *The Continuity of American Poetry.* Princeton, N.J.: Princeton University Press, 1961.

Perloff, Marjorie. "Charles Olson and the 'Inferior Predecessors': 'Projective Verse' Revisited." *ELH* 40 (1973): 285–306.

Philip, J. B. "Charles Olson Reconsidered." *Journal of American Studies* 5 (1971): 293–305.

Philipson, Morris. *Outline of a Jungian Aesthetics.* Evanston, Ill.: Northwestern University Press, 1963.

Plutarch. *Morals.* Translated by C. W. King. London: George Bell and Sons, 1908.

Pound, Ezra, ed. *The Chinese Written Character as a Medium for Poetry.* San Francisco: City Lights Books, 1936.

———. *Literary Essays of Ezra Pound.* New York: New Directions, 1968.

Richards, I. A. *Mencius on the Mind.* London: Routledge & Kegan Paul, 1964.

Rosenthal, M. L. *The New Poets: American and British Poetry Since World War II.* New York: Oxford University Press, 1967.

———. "Olson/his Poetry." *The Massachusetts Review* 12 (1971): 45–57.

Sauer, Carl Ortwin. *Land and Life.* Edited by John Leighly. Berkeley, Calif.: University of California Press, 1967.

Seelye, Catherine, ed. *Charles Olson & Ezra Pound: An Encounter at St. Elizabeths.* New York: Grossman Publishers, 1975.

Snow, Wilbert. "A Teacher's View." *Massachusetts Review* 12 (1971): 40–44.

Sorrentino, Gilbert. "Black Mountaineering." *Poetry* 116 (1970): 110–20.

Stepanchev, Stephen. *American Poetry Since 1945.* New York: Harper & Row, 1965.

Sutton, Walter. *American Free Verse: The Modern Revolution in Poetry.* New York: New Directions, 1973.

Thompson, Sir Eric. *Civilization of the Mayas.* 4th ed. No. 25. Field Museum of Natural History. Chicago: University of Chicago Department of Anthropology, 1942.

von Hallberg, Robert. "Olson's Relation to Pound and Williams." *Contemporary Literature* 15 (1974): 15–48.

———. "Olson, Whitehead, and the Objectivists." *Boundary 2* 2 (1973–74): 85–111.

———. *The Scholar's Art.* Cambridge, Mass.: Harvard University Press.

Walsh, Chad. "Introduction." *Poetry and Truth.* Edited by George Butterick. San Francisco: Four Seasons Foundation, 1971.

Weyl, Hermann. *The Philosophy of Mathematics and Natural Science.* Princeton, N.J.: Princeton University Press, 1949.

Wheelwright, Philip, trans. *Heraclitus.* Princeton, N.J.: Princeton University Press, 1959.

Whitehead, Alfred North. *Process and Reality.* New York: Macmillan Co., 1929.

Wiener, Norbert. *Cybernetics; or, Control and Communication in the Animal and the Machine.* 2d ed. Cambridge, Mass.: M.I.T. Press, 1961.

———. *The Human Use of Human Beings: Cybernetics and Society.* Boston: Houghton Mifflin Co., 1950.

Wilhelm, Richard, ed. and trans. *The Secret of the Golden Flower: A Chinese Book of Life.* Rev. ed. New York: Harcourt, Brace & World, 1962.

Williams, William Carlos. *Paterson.* Norfolk, Conn.: New Directions, 1963.

Index